The Reference Shelf

Corporate Power in the United States

Edited by Joseph Sora

The Reference Shelf
Volume 70 • Number 3

The H. W. Wilson Company
New York • Dublin
1998

Reference Shelf

The books in this series contain reprints of articles, excerpts from books, addresses on current issues, and studies of social trends in the United States and other countries. There are six separately bound numbers in each volume, all of which are usually published in the same calendar year. Numbers one through five are each devoted to a single subject, providing background information and discussion from various points of view and concluding with a subject index and comprehensive bibliography that lists books, pamphlets, and abstracts of additional articles on the subject. The final number of each volume is a collection of recent speeches, and it contains a cumulative speaker index. Books in the series may be purchased individually or on subscription.

Visit H.W. Wilson's web site: www.hwwilson.com

Library of Congress Cataloging-in-Publication Data

Corporate Power in the U.S./edited by Joseph Sora
p. cm.—(Reference shelf; v. 70, no.3)
Includes bibliography references and index.
ISBN 0-8242-0943-5
1. Coporations—United States. I. Sora, Joseph W. II. Series.
HD2785.C585 1998 98-8162
338.7'4'0973—dc21 CIP

Cover: Executives discuss stock prices.
Photo: AP/Wide World Photos

Printed in the United States of America

Contents

IV. The Corporation and the Media

Bibliography

Preface

At this point in American history, the large corporation maintains a very strong presence on the national landscape. Perhaps this is because most of the working population spends their day at a corporation that employs more than 1,000 people. Corporate power could also be a consequence of the corporation's impact upon the economy—over half of all sales receipts are generated by a large corporation. Nor can we discount the sheer (albeit often masked) presence of the corporation. Staggering levels of both print and broadcast advertising, corporate ownership of everything from sports teams to Web sites, and the creation of the products and services we purchase all combine to push the corporation to the forefront of the American consciousness.

The corporation is thus a force that enjoys an unprecedented amount of power. While many argue that such power is a natural extension of the capitalism that has always defined the American economic system, corporate power is questioned and accepted, condemned and praised. The articles in this issue of *The Reference Shelf* articulate the level of power attained by the American corporation, as well as the debate such acquisition of power continues to evoke. By reading the articles contained herein, it is clear that the corporation maintains an extensive and complicated presence in the United States that warrants serious and studied discussion.

Beginning with an article that traces the corporation from medieval times to its present state, the first section in this compilation, The American Corporation, strives to define the corporation, convey gauges of its power, and portray the defining characteristics of corporate power in late-20th-century America. From these articles it is clear that the quest to control corporate power enjoys as rich a history as the corporations themselves. Yet despite the populist tradition of combating corporate power, the American corporation thrives and is currently achieving a global presence. Recent technological advances have, no doubt, facilitated the expansion of the corporation. While many fear and lament such expansion, others welcome it as a source of both increased revenues and new challenges.

The second section, The Corporate Presence, articulates corporate power as it is manifest through the sheer presence of the corporation. The corporation is such a prolific entity that it is becoming difficult to go anywhere without seeing some reminder of a corporation. No longer associated with merely a single, identifying product, corporations, in one form or another, have permeated what we see, what we hear, where we walk, what we say, and, as many argue, what we want to be. While the corporate presence is only an indirect testament to the corporation's power, it is a direct testament to the impact of the corporation's effect upon the culture-at-large.

As noted, corporations control vast amounts of wealth. Along with such wealth inevitably lies power. Section III, The Corporate Gift, discusses the power of the corporation which results from the money the corporation donates to a variety of entities, ranging from charities to political parties. Inherent to any discussion of corporate donations is a questioning of the motives behind those donations, including, do corporations give money purely for the benefit of the recipient or are there ulterior motives?

Should the corporation donate indiscriminately or target those that are clearly akin to their market base? Should a political party accept money from the corporation when such acceptance may entail placing the corporation's interest above the interest of the constituency?

The last section of this compilation, The Corporation and the Media, is concerned with the recent corporate domination of information sources, be they news-oriented or not. For our purposes, the effect of such ownership is really a calling into question of the extent to which corporate agendas and priorities will affect the integrity and quality of the information that is published or broadcast. While many believe that consolidating newspapers, publishing houses, and television programs under common corporate ownership is an inherent threat to free speech and truth in reporting, others believe it to be an inconsequential reality. Nonetheless, as the corporation involves itself with what we read and hear it bolsters its own power over what we know.

It is hoped that these articles will prompt the reader to take a closer look at the presence of the corporation within America. The issue is by no means clear-cut, and should be examined within the many contexts the corporation has injected its presence. The editor of this volume of *The Reference Shelf* would like to thank Michael Schulze for his trust, Frank McGuckin for his tireless work toward the creation of a solid publication, and Irene Astorga for her patience, kindness, and inspired talent.

Joseph Sora
May 1998

I. The American Corporation

Editor's Introduction

The formation of the country and of the modern-day corporation occurred as hand-in-hand processes, supplementing and complementing one another since the early days of our Republic. From this intertwining, the corporation emerged with a dual identity. On the one hand, it provides mass employment and profoundly adds to the country's material and economic wealth. During the 19th century, corporations laid the railroads that allowed America to capitalize on its inherent wealth. Now, we can thank corporations such as Microsoft and IBM for universally granting us access to technology's cutting edge. On the other hand, the fear of the corporation's political and financial power lay tangent to the corporate advancement America has historically profited by. Such fear has aroused not only voiced protest and calls for tighter corporate regulation, but targeted legislation as well. Corporate power is thus subject to conflicted views: both admired for its fruits, and checked and monitored to prohibit potential tyranny. The aim of Section I is to provide an overview of corporate power, its assets and liabilities, its detractors and its supporters.

The first article in this section discusses the history of the corporation in America. According to the author, Professor Morton Keller, the corporation "turned out to be as American as apple pie" perhaps because the concept of the corporation democratizes the access to wealth and power that had formerly been reserved for the aristocratic classes. By the 1850s, just about anyone could incorporate themselves and attempt to scale the financial heights. Yet "anticorporate strictures" also have a deep history in America. According to Keller, the history of the corporation is, in part, a tension between the quest to advance and the need to balance and distribute the power that necessarily comes with such advancement.

"Measuring Corporate Power: Assessing the Options" is an academic paper that delineates the yardsticks used to gauge corporate power. According to the author, while many marvel at the corporation's general attainment of power, few understand that power on a specific and manageable level. In this article, the author describes those "variables" that he believes provide the most accurate measurement of a corporation's true power. They include corporate executives who serve on the boards of many corporations, "the percentage of the labor force that is unionized," and the extent to which a corporation dominates a particular industry.

Once a corporation's power has been defined, strategies for monitoring that power abound. While many advocate government regulation, including antitrust legislation, others argue that the corporation itself can in fact act responsibly without the enforcement of government. The following two articles discuss potential checks on corporate power. In "Corporate Accountability" Ralph D. Ward argues that given the "large scale corporate governance" that he believes will soon be a reality, corporate boards, being the body of individuals to whom senior management reports, must be made responsible for the actions of the company. Ward contends that the board of directors defines the corporation's use of power, particularly in regard to "the greater public welfare." In essence, Ward argues for a check on corporate boards that is meant to foster greater corporate accountability and, therefore, responsibility.

As Ward discusses a possible way the corporation can restrain itself, Eleanor M. Fox gives a quick rundown of government's regulation of corporate power, both past and present. After recalling legislation by both Theodore Roosevelt and F.D.R. meant to limit corporate power, Fox argues that as American corporations become global forces, the spirit of the Roosevelts' antitrust efforts has been lost. Recalling a concern raised by Keller in "The Making of the Modern Corporation," Fox hopes that as corporations expand their reach and become transnational forces, we will not compromise our restraints upon them.

Thanks in large part to technology, corporate globalization is in fact the defining effort of the American corporation in the late 20th century. While Fox worries globalization may extend corporate power beyond restraint, Jay Mandle, author of "The Good Side of Going Global," asserts that the benefit of extending American corporate power beyond our borders far outweighs the threat of unimpinged corporate power. According to Mandle, the value of globalization is evidenced by the modernization, in the form of increased production capabilities, that the American corporation imparts to less developed nations. In addition, corporate globalization challenges our workers to be "successful participants in the world economy." From this article, we learn that there are also benefits to the American corporate structure. Just as corporate power, in part, maintains America's position as a world leader, it can also raise the standard of living in less-developed nations.

The Making of the Modern Corporation[1]

The large business corporation has a firm place in the American imagination as the dark repository of private power. There are no more reliable villains on TV or in movieland than these shadowy, soulless, omnipresent institutions and the faceless, greedy men and women who serve them. And yet today as much as ever before, corporations are accepted as the driving engines of our economy, as the places where most of us work. It sometimes seems that corporations in America are what lying was to the English schoolgirl: an abomination unto the Lord, but an ever-reliable friend in time of trouble.

The corporate charter was invented in medieval Europe. For centuries, incorporation legitimated a variety of public institutions and semiprivate enterprises, rather than private businesses. It found receptive soil in the American colonies, and during the early years of the Republic became a widely accessible instrument of economic growth. Yet from early on there was a tension between the public character and private purposes of corporations.

As the term *corporation* became a synonym for big business after the late 19th century, corporations increasingly became the subject of political debate and the target of legislation and regulation. But to an extent that is not generally appreciated, many of the challenges posed by the corporate form have been handled in the nation's courtrooms rather than in the political arena. In part, this is simply because corporations are creatures of the law. But turning the corporation to public purposes without impinging on its proven ability to create wealth (which is, in fact, another public purpose) has proved also to be a very delicate task—one of many such tasks that Americans have relied heavily upon the courts to carry out.

To understand what corporations are, it is necessary first to have some idea of where they came from. The idea that certain kinds of institutions—towns, guilds, schools, hospitals—should have a charter from some higher authority that grants them defined privileges dates from at least the Middle Ages. Early charters were variants of the basic feudal contract that linked lords and vassals in medieval society; if for individuals, then why not for institutions?

Out of this experience came the idea of chartering commercial ventures as well. During the 16th and 17th centuries, English entrepreneurs sought royal charters for all sorts of ventures,

---

[1] Article by Morton Keller, Spector professor of history at Brandeis University, editor of *The Encyclopedia of the United States Congress* (1995), and the author of several books, including *Regulating a New Economy: Public Policy and Economic Change in America*, 1900–1933 (1990). From *The Wilson Quarterly* 21/4:58-69 Autumn 1997.

including trading outposts in the Baltic, Russia, and Ireland, and then "plantations" in the New World.

Most of these early chartered ventures were joint-stock companies, composed of investors who pooled their assets for a single enterprise. The Dutch East India Company of 1602 is often accounted the first true stock corporation, with a permanent fund of capital. The great advantage here was that in the (not unlikely) event of failure, the participants' liability was limited to the amount they had invested. This made it easier to amass the large capital pools these early overseas ventures required.

So the early modern corporation emerged to meet the financial and organizational needs of the Age of Discovery. But charters also served the power-aggrandizing monarchs of 17th century England, such as James I. By establishing the principle that corporations were legal entities created by the Crown, the king not only asserted his authority over them but was in a position to grant monopolies and other perquisites to his favorites.

"Partnerships made sense in a tightly knit, hierarchical society..."

But the royal stamp of approval, too freely given, encouraged rampant speculation, much as U.S. government deposit insurance in the 1980s encouraged American savings and loan societies to overextend themselves. The inevitable end came in 1720 with the ruinous collapse of the South Sea and Mississippi "bubbles," rampages of speculation in the shares of two companies established to launch commercial ventures in the New World. Parliament's Bubble Act of that year put an end to almost all corporate chartering for commercial purposes in England for the rest of the 18th century.

That long hiatus, coming as it did during the seedtime of the Industrial Revolution, strengthened what was already a strong inclination in England to rely on partnerships rather than corporations as the preferred form of business enterprise. Partnerships made sense in a tightly knit, hierarchical society, where extensive and complicated bonds of personal relationship defined the social structure and controlled the major sources of investment capital.

The Bubble Act applied also to the American colonies, which faced the added difficulty of trying to launch commercial ventures in the face of a British imperial policy that reserved the profits of more sophisticated forms of enterprise to the mother country. The Philadelphia Contributionship for Insuring Houses from Loss by Fire (1768) was the only chartered business corporation in colonial America, acceptable because of the socially useful nature of its business.

Nevertheless, incorporation turned out to be as American as apple pie. Every colony had a royal charter by the eve of the Revolution. Colleges, charities, New England towns and villages, churches, and quasi-public enterprises such as wharves and mills eagerly sought charters of incorporation from colonial assemblies.

Independence opened the floodgates to innovation in many realms of American society, not least the launching of commercial ventures. No longer did a hostile king or parliament threaten their legitimacy. And a new structure of state and national government now existed that could create, define, and limit incorporation.

An important early statement on the place of the charter in the American system of government was John Marshall's decision in the *Dartmouth College* case (1819). Could New Hampshire unilaterally alter the terms of Dartmouth's pre-Revolution royal charter? Marshall (and a dutifully unanimous Supreme Court) said no: Dartmouth's charter was a contract, and hence came under the protective wing of the Constitution's clause barring the impairment of contract.

This ruling seemed to suggest that incorporated bodies would enjoy a high level of immunity from state interference. New York judge James Kent said soon after the *Dartmouth College* decision that it "did more than any other single act...to throw an impregnable barrier around all rights and franchises derived from the grant of government; and to give solidity and inviolability to the literary, charitable, religious and commercial institutions of our country."

But to say that a charter was the same as a contract challenged the assumption in English common law that a corporation was free to do everything that it was not explicitly forbidden to do. Instead, American courts took the view that a corporation could do only what its charter—granted by the state legislature, that republican tribune of the people–explicitly said it could do. In other words, a charter was not an open-ended grant of authority but a specific and limited authorization to take on a particular task: an approach well suited to a republic dedicated to the principles of limited and representative government.

There was more. By saying that corporate charters were contracts, not grants, the Supreme Court stripped away any implication that corporations enjoyed the special favor of the chartering authority. It thus enabled the charter of incorporation to become a widely accessible instrument in the contract-dominated market economy of the 19th century.

The benefits of the corporate device quickly became evident. Incorporation's limited liability reduced investor risk, thus making it easier to attract the relatively large and unaffiliated American investing public. And a corporate structure made it easier to bring in professional management. These were important advantages in a scattered, diverse society, so unlike the tightly interconnected world of business and capital in England.

The spread of corporations also democratized—or, more accurately, republicanized—commercial enterprise by bringing it within the framework of American government. Charters came not from an unaccountable sovereign but from popularly elected state legislatures. At the same time, the semiofficial status of corporate charters eased the access of companies—and their competitors—to the new nation's legislatures and courts.

In the heady days of the early and mid-19th century, American corporate chartering expanded as never before. Schools and colleges, medical and agricultural and charitable societies, churches, towns, and cities barraged state legislatures with charter requests. The number of business corporations soared. By 1817 some 2,000 had been chartered, and this was just the beginning. Turnpikes, canals, bridges, banks, ferries, steamboat and insurance companies, and railroads were the most conspicuous recipients. New York alone granted about 500 turnpike charters between 1797 and 1847.

The prevailing view was that there was no important difference between purely commercial and quasi-public enterprises. Each in its own way benefited the young republic. It was not difficult to believe that banks, bridges, canals, turnpikes, railroads, and insurance companies played a public role, and to accept the fact that they often got special privileges, such as monopoly rights for a period of years, when they were chartered.

"The depression of the late 1830s and early '40s...cleared the way for new ideas about the scope and meaning of incorporation."

But as the economy grew, these privileges came under fire. Some critics were rising entrepreneurs who sought to compete with existing enterprises, while others voiced a more general resentment that these "artificial creatures" should be so favored by the state. "Corporations have neither bodies to be kicked, nor souls to be damned," went a common complaint of the time.

The depression of the late 1830s and early '40s, which led to massive failures of canal and railroad companies, cleared the way for new ideas about the scope and meaning of incorporation. One result was easier access. By the mid-19th century, legislatures were passing general laws designed to make incorporation as cheap and easy as possible. No longer was it necessary to secure a legislative act. Now one filled out a simple form and paid a small fee. Incorporation became almost a perquisite of American citizenship, like voting or going to school. This democratization of what had once been an instrument of privilege made the corporation a form of economic organization more widely used in the United States than anywhere else in the Western world. In New York, for instance, more than 4,700 manufacturing firms were chartered between 1848 and 1866.

At the same time, the ability of the state (if it so chose) to regulate corporations was reinforced. The Supreme Court's *Charles River Bridge* decision (1837) set the tone. Writing for the majority, Chief Justice Roger B. Taney refused to let the privileges granted to an 18th-cenhury Massachusetts bridge company block the construction of a second bridge nearby, even if the effect of the new enterprise was to destroy the economic advantage of the old one. The promise of economic growth lay not in the guarantee of old privileges (as Marshall had suggested in the *Dartmouth College* case) but in a process of "creative destruction" in which existing charter rights were narrowly interpreted in their duration and impact, and legislatures were empowered to foster economic change at the expense of vested corporate interests.

States that freely granted the gift of incorporation were ready to regulate or limit what they created. A number of them (including New York in its 1846 constitution) forbade subsidies or favors of any form to railroads and other corporations. While the courts remained sensitive to the sanctity of property and contract, they tended to interpret corporate charters narrowly; in effect, to say to a company that wanted to go beyond its prescribed powers, "Have you got it in writing?" It was common for corporate charters to include a reserve clause allowing the legislature to amend them at any time. And by the 1850s, the "police power" to regulate the safety, health, morals, and welfare of the people had come to be accepted in American law as a broad justification for economic regulation.

This, then, was the ambiguous status of the business corporation in the mid-19th century, on the eve of the rise of big business. The corporate charter had evolved into a readily accessible instrument for a vibrant entrepreneurial society. Simply and cheaply attained, stripped of its traditional exclusionary or monopoly character, it was an essential handmaiden of economic growth. But at the same time, the corporation had an aura of threatening economic power to which government was expected to respond.

The first corporate body to evoke such fears was the Second Bank of the United States. But it died in 1832, when President Andrew Jackson vetoed the bill rechartering it. Next came the railroads. By the mid-19th century they had become the nation's first big business, a new and frightening source of unchecked power. In the early 1870s E. L. Godkin of the *Nation* observed, in his usual portentous way: "The locomotive is coming in contact with the framework of our institutions. In this country of simple government, the most powerful centralizing force which civilization has yet produced must, within the next score years, assume its relations to that political machinery which is to control and regulate it."

Popular anxiety over corporate power peaked at the turn of the century with the movement against "the trusts." In the late 1870s, John D. Rockefeller's attorney Samuel C. T. Dodd figured out a way for Standard Oil to absorb competitors without running afoul of its Ohio charter, which forbade it from holding the stock of other companies. The stock of Standard Oil and the companies it absorbed was turned over to a Rockefeller-dominated board of trustees, which issued trust certificates in return. A trust was not a corporation, and thus no state laws were broken.

Only about 10 trusts were launched during the 1880s. But the potential for more such mergers, and the fearsome business practices of the Standard Oil combine, made the trust a lightning rod for public concern over corporations and big business. The author of an 1883 law journal article wondered, "The Standard

Oil has grown to be a more powerful—corporation, shall we call it? or what? for this is one of our questions—than any other below the national government itself." A number of states passed antitrust laws, and in 1890 the Sherman Antitrust Act, which outlawed "every contract, combination in the form of trust or otherwise, or conspiracy in restraint of trade or commerce," swept through Congress.

But this legislation hardly eased the growing national concern over big business. In its early years, the Sherman Act proved to be difficult to administer. The Supreme Court, in the *Sugar Trust* case (1893), severely limited the impact of the law by ruling that although the American Sugar Refining Company controlled more than 90 percent of the nation's output, it could not be attacked under the Sherman Act. Why? Because sugar refining was part of the manufacturing process, a concern of the chartering state; the federal government's authority applied only after the company's product began moving in interstate commerce.

"From 1898 to 1902 there were 2,653 mergers, with a combined capitalization of $6.3 billion."

At the same time James B. Dill, another creative corporation lawyer—it was soon after this that Finley Peter Dunne's Mr. Dooley observed that what looked like a stone wall to the ordinary man was a triumphal arch to the lawyer—came up with a new legal device that nicely removed the remaining constraints on corporate consolidation. Dill's invention was the holding company: a corporation whose sole reason for being was to possess the stock of other corporations.

What to do about state laws that forbade corporations from doing this? That was easy: get a state or two to ease that restriction, and then interstate competitiveness would do the rest. Delaware and New Jersey soon obliged in response to intensive corporate lobbying and became the legal homes of many of America's largest corporations. The result, said one observer, was that "the conduct and condition of [a corporation's] business are treated as private and not public affairs."

This legal-legislative transformation went hand in hand with a new judicial perception of the corporation. In its *Santa Clara* decision of 1886 the Supreme Court held, en passant, that a corporation was a person under the Fourteenth Amendment and thus was entitled to the guarantees of due process and equal protection that the amendment afforded to the nation's citizens. This quiet change sculpted a constitutional safeguard of the rights of newly freed slaves into a potent instrument for use against state taxation and regulation.

It is not surprising that large American corporations felt free to go on a consolidation binge around the turn of the century. From 1898 to 1902 there were 2,653 mergers, with a combined capitalization of $6.3 billion. Within a few years an economy dominated by large, consolidated railroad, coal, steel, tobacco, oil, and dozens of other giant firms—the world of the 20th century American economy—had come into being.

Europe was creating its own economic megaliths at the same

time: Great Britain saw 198 mergers during 1898–1900. But very different political, economic, and strategic realities prevailed there. Partnerships continued to be the rule in Britain (though they enjoyed limited liability and other corporate goodies). And English courts saw nothing wrong with—indeed, encouraged—firms entering into cartel agreements on prices and production. As an observer of the time put it, "Combination has been accepted without regulation in England because the entire English social system is a series of closed groups." Nothing of this sort was legal in the United States.

The popular American response to the rise of big business was colored by very different social realities. American historical memory did not include sentimentalized feudal-aristocratic traditions of patriarchal oversight, or guilds that were part of a traditional social order, or a tradition of class conflict. Rather, the most powerful economic creeds were individualism and self-reliance; enterprise was not to be cosseted but was to be left alone by the state. The growing diversity of early-20th-century American life—with manufacturers, merchants, farmers, railroads, shippers, retailers, consumers, unions, lawyers, judges, economists, journalists, and politicians pushing their interests and jockeying for position—served only to strengthen this fluid social environment.

In theory, Americans could draw on several different policy responses to the rise of big business. One was public ownership of public utilities. Another was federal incorporation (and therefore oversight)—sometimes sought by industry leaders themselves, who saw in it protection from burdensome state supervision. Yet a third was general federal regulation of industrial prices and services: the creation of an interstate trade commission to parallel the railroads' Interstate Commerce Commission.

But these alternatives failed to suit the national temperament—or to fit the prevailing realities in American politics and government. Public ownership of utilities was tried in a few places, but the opposition of private interests and public suspicion of politician-run enterprises kept it marginal. Presidents Theodore Roosevelt and William Howard Taft proposed federal chartering, without success. And while the Federal Trade Commission was created in 1914, it did little more than try to block false and deceptive advertising.

What developed instead was a heavily judicial and highly nonideological system of mixed state and federal oversight, dominated by the federal courts. The number of antitrust suits varied from presidential administration to administration. But in the last analysis, antitrust policy was not set by elected officials or the government bureaucracy. It was set by the Supreme Court.

What was the character of that judicial policy? At first, reluctance to use the Sherman Act to strike down large combinations. Then, influenced in part by political and public opinion, a growing readiness to order the dissolution of combines that clearly violated the letter and spirit of the Sherman Act, culminating in the *Standard Oil* and *American Tobacco* decisions of 1911. In these cases, the Court set down a "rule of reason" for judging when combinations and bigness passed over the invisible line from efficiency to monopoly—and it ruled that both companies had done so. But the decisions made it plain that it would be the *Court*, and not an administrative or political agency, that would decide when that line had been crossed.

There were other forms of corporate regulation besides court-driven antitrust policy, but none were very satisfactory. Insurance companies, banks, and securities markets were subject to state regulatory systems—all notable for their inadequacy. Railroads, regulated by the Interstate Commerce Commission since 1887, were involved for decades in an intricate, politically charged, and terribly costly regulatory drama.

"Easy access to the corporate form was now a century old, and taken for granted."

The newer public utilities—gas and electric, bus and streetcar and telephone companies—operated in yet another distinct regulatory environment. They were expected to provide a constant flow of a necessary service, and by their very nature they were monopolies, or nearly so. To deal with then, the states resurrected the old regulatory device of licensing. Public service or utility commissions issued "certificates of public convenience and necessity" to the companies under their supervision: a new form of corporate oversight. But often these commissions were "captured" by the utilities they regulated.

None of these problems reduced the ubiquity of the corporate form of business organization. Big business was only the tip of the American corporate iceberg. The vast majority of corporations were small enterprises, remote from the regulatory world of antitrust or utilities regulation. Easy access to the corporate form was now a century old, and taken for granted. There were more than 340,000 corporations in 1916 and 516,000 in 1931, when they controlled some 30 percent of the nation's wealth and accounted for four-fifths of business income. No one worried that hundreds of thousands of farmers, shopkeepers, and small manufacturers availed themselves of the liability and, increasingly in the 20th century, the tax advantages of incorporation.

What did continue to concern courts, legislatures, and (intermittently) the public was how to restrict the corporation's potential for economic and political power while not crippling its potential for economic growth. This involved, first of all, an assault on the late-19th-century legal doctrine that a corporation was the equivalent of a person. That doctrine was the source of some of the more controversial judicial decisions of the early 20th century. It allowed corporations to claim Fourteenth Amendment immunity from much state taxation, and to beat back some attempts to regulate wages and working conditions. Companies argued with some success that the states had no right to interfere with the contracts that they as "persons" entered into with their workers.

Not until the 1930s did the Supreme Court finally come to accept that both the federal government and the states should have considerable regulatory authority over corporations. Congress then passed laws severely limiting the ability of employers to secure court injunctions against strikers and guaranteeing collective bargaining. Corporate taxation increased significantly during the New Deal and World War II. Big business came once again, as in the Progressive era, to be treated as what in fact it was: not a collection of legal "persons" more or less free to do what they would, but a potent American institution.

The decades since the 1930s have not fundamentally altered the place of the corporation in American life. Antitrust now, as throughout the 20th century, ebbs and flows with the forces of politics and the economy. Comparing the breakup of Standard Oil in 1911 and of AT&T a decade ago gives one an overpowering sense of *déjà vu*. The anticorporate strictures of Ralph Nader and other latter-day critics stand in a tradition that has its roots in the early 19th century. True, there is far more regulation of corporations today, including rules on environmental and occupational safety and health. And modern liability law makes companies much more subject to consumer and bystander damage suits than in the past. Yet big business today has as secure a place in American society as at any time during the past century.

One feature of large corporations has been a continuing source of trouble: the separation of ownership and control. Until the 20th century, ownership rested in relatively few hands—though rarely in the hands of only one proprietor, such as Henry Ford—and owners were able for the most part to exercise effective control. But as companies grew bigger, and stockholders more numerous (4.4 million in 1900, an estimated 18 million in 1928), the separation of control from ownership loomed ever larger. In 1927 and 1929 leading New York corporation lawyers revised Delaware's statutes, already hospitable enough to make that state the home of 70,000 firms, further strengthening the hand of management against stockholders.

The Modern Corporation and Private Property (1932), by lawyer (and later New Deal brain truster) Adolf Berle and economist Gardiner Means, addressed the ownership-control problem in much the same way as, a generation before, Louis D. Brandeis's *Other People's Money* (1914) focused on corporate consolidation and size. Could stockholder-owners who were not actually responsible for the operation of a firm justly claim all of its profits? And given the impossibility of oversight by masses of stockholders, how could non-owner managers be counted on to maximize profits and secure the health of the company, rather than seek perquisites and power for themselves?

Berle and Means's larger point was that corporations were social as well as economic institutions and thus subject to public accountability. It took the Great Depression and the New Deal to bring about significant reform, though nowhere near as comprehensive as many corporate critics wanted. The Securities Act of 1933 and the Securities Exchange Act of 1934 imposed strict new rules on stock issues and securities trading, and required full disclosure of executive compensation. State securities laws were also tightened.

But the gap between stockholders and management persisted. Stockholders continued to be regarded more as investors than as owners—and, indeed, it is hard to see how any other assumption could work. "Faith in publicity," the sovereign Progressive remedy (along with antitrust) for corporate ills, has remained the guiding spirit of corporation law reform. In times of corporate profitability (that is, pretty much since the Great Depression), criticism of the management-stockholder relationship—like criticism of corporate size—tends to be muted. Even today's excessive stock options, golden parachutes, and other arrangements that avaricious managers secure with the help of complaisant directors elicit more indignation than action. Of course, an economic catastrophe could very well change that.

"Corporations seldom form a united political front, and big business is often vulnerable to adverse public opinion."

Two very different impressions emerge from the long history of the corporation in the United States. One is that the corporate form has been extraordinarily useful as a way of giving legal (and public) standing to economic or social ventures. Whether in regard to a covenanted New England town in the 17th century, a colonial college in the 18th century, a bank or a railroad company in the 19th century, or the biggest of big businesses in the 20th century, some form of incorporation has been a sine qua non. It guarantees public standing or limited liability, helps attract capital, or gives managers relatively free scope to operate.

No less striking is the halting and uncertain, slow and limited record of the state and of public opinion when it comes to subjecting corporations to significant government control. The usual explanation is that big business wields enormous political power. No one would deny the existence of that power, but it seems an insufficient explanation. Corporations seldom form a united political front, and big business is often vulnerable to adverse public opinion. The antitrust movement of the early 20th century, the New Deal, and the continuing strain of populist hostility to big business are all evidence of that. In American politics, an aroused public that knows what it wants usually can get its way.

It is revealing that the area in which modern corporations have been most vulnerable to public control is liability law. Customers or bystanders who suffer harm from a company's products, even if the harm was impossible to anticipate, now routinely win multimillion-dollar judgments against corporate giants. It is no accident that this is an area, like antitrust, that is the particular responsibility of the courts. Corporations to a considerable degree are legal creatures, and it is the law, more than politics or government, that seems best able to trace the bounds between their private rights and public responsibilities.

Much of the corporation's relative immunity from broad political assault exists because it has been able to lay claim to the status—and the legitimacy—that comes from being an old, massive, generally successful American institution. The corporate device is used by middling farmers and entrepreneurs as well as gargantuan businesses. And despite highly publicized episodes of downsizing, many big companies still command the loyalty of their managers and workers. Corporations, as has so often been observed, are social as well as economic institutions, and the attractive power of the corporate culture should not be underestimated. Most of all, corporations, especially large ones, have been able to deliver the economic goods. For all their very evident faults and inadequacies, as long as they continue to do that, their place in American society seems assured.

Measuring Corporate Power: Assessing the Options[2]

Institutional economists have long argued that corporate power is a growing and insidious phenomenon. Corporations, beyond their ability to manipulate output and resource prices, exert significant control over government policies and household living standards. With labor's power declining as corporate power has grown, working conditions, real wages, and the distribution of income have all deteriorated.

While the literature is replete with explanations for the existence and consequences of corporate power, far less has been achieved in the area of measuring corporate power. Much of the institutionalist work on measurement has focused on the inadequacy of existing measures. This is an important step, but the success of these efforts only serves to illuminate the need to identify new, more viable measures.

This paper investigates a number of potentially valid measures of corporate power. The purpose of this paper is not to identify definitively the best method of measurement, but rather to expand the existing dialogue and to move the discipline closer to the step of integrating the phenomenon of corporate power into empirically testable hypotheses.

While few agree on the best way to measure corporate power, most concur that an accurate gauge will necessarily be complex. The lines of causality and effect between the sources and consequences of power are multidirectional. Profits, for example, are a means of expanding power, which in turn may expand a corporation's profitability. As William Shepherd asserts, the process is difficult to visualize and far more difficult to measure. Nevertheless, the difficulty of the task does not diminish its importance or our responsibility for pursuing it.

Assessing which variables are plausible measures of corporate power involves both theoretical and practical considerations. Variables considered by this paper include: (1) industry concentration ratios; (2) aggregate concentration ratios; (3) number of corporate interlocks as a percentage of the number of corporations; (4) after-tax corporate profits as a percentage of personal or national income; (5) the ratio of the marginal product of labor to the real wage; (6) the percentage of total government revenue derived from corporate income taxes; and (7) the percentage of the labor force that is unionized.

---

[2] Article by Randy R. Grant, assistant professor of economics, Linfield College, McMinnville, Oregon, presented at the annual meeting of the Association for Evolutionary Economics, in New Orleans, Louisiana, on January 4–6, 1997. From *Journal of Economic Issues* 31/2:451-458 Je '97.

Specific Variables Considered

Industry Concentration Ratios

In comparing the degree of market power possessed in different sectors, industry concentration ratios are frequently employed. These ratios indicate industry share "controlled" by the largest firms. The four-firm concentration ratio is the one most frequently employed.

Gaps in the available data are a primary obstacle to conducting a reliable time series investigation of this measure. Even if the required data were available, the extent and impacts of conglomeration still would not be captured by such a measure. As William Dugger and others have argued, the U.S. economy is controlled not only by corporations, but by conglomerates. A conglomerate is a legally organized and managed collection of otherwise unrelated firms operating in unrelated industries and markets. When firms merge or are acquired by conglomerates, power may become more concentrated into the hands of fewer firms and directors. However, because companies within a conglomerate participate in different industries, conglomeration would not necessarily change concentration ratios.

"It is estimated that in the 1960s, 80 percent of mergers were 'conglomerate'..."

Despite merger waves in the 1960s and 1980s, Dugger observes that concentration ratios have changed little for several decades. He argues that the numbers fail to reveal increases in corporate power. Dugger adds that as conglomerates expand and exercise more power, concentration ratios "become increasingly less relevant as measures of economic power." It is estimated that in the 1960s, 80 percent of mergers were "conglomerate," involving neither horizontal nor vertical integration of firms.

Industry concentration ratios also ignore the impact of foreign competition. Thus, the four-firm ratio for an industry could be rising, reflecting increased dominance of the domestic market by the four largest firms. At the same time, however, these four largest firms could be losing market share to foreign competition. The result is that the concentration ratios would rise, while the overall market power of the largest firms was falling. Under those circumstances, concentration ratios would incorrectly measure changes in the power of domestic corporations.

Aggregate Concentration Ratios

Perhaps the most popular enlisting measure of corporate power is the aggregate concentration ratio. Aggregate concentration ratios measure the percentage of sales, assets, and value added that are controlled by the largest 50, 100, 200, or 500 firms in the economy. Higher percentages signify greater concentration and suggest increased consolidation of power. Although of some use, concentration ratios are an inadequate barometer of corporate power.

Aggregate concentration ratios fail to provide information

about non-manufacturing businesses. Increased concentration in banking and agriculture, while likely reflecting greater corporate power, is not captured in the aggregate concentration ratios. As the manufacturing sector declines in size relative to other sectors in the economy, aggregate concentration ratios become less meaningful as a measure of corporate power.

Another shortcoming of aggregate concentration ratios is that they, like industry concentration ratios, fail to account for foreign competition. Aggregate concentration ratios measure only the domestic shares of industrial activity and fail to account for changes in foreign market share. As foreign competition for market share intensifies, aggregate concentration ratios that include only domestic firms become increasingly inadequate measures of corporate power.

Even if aggregate concentration ratios could be defended as reliable measures of corporate power, the reality is that the data are not complete enough to conduct a useful time series analysis.

Corporate Interlocks/Interlocking Directorates

One means of dealing with the issue of conglomeration is to measure the number of corporate interlocks. As John Scott...defines it, an *interlock* is "the social relation that is created between two enterprises when one person is a member of the Board of Directors in each enterprise." Scott also observes that the workings of interlocks serve an important function in determining the economic and social power of corporations, and yet they often go unnoticed.

It is generally assumed that a positive relationship exists between the number of interlocks a company has and the size and power of the firm. While this appears to be valid for most individual firms, it is fallacious to conclude that an increase in the aggregate number of interlocks in an economy must therefore signify an overall increase in corporate power. In fact, the opposite may be the case. An increase in the number of interlocks could result from an increased number of corporations. If an increase in the number of corporations results in more competition among firms, then we would expect the power of corporations, both individually and collectively, to be diminished.

The creation of interlocks does not, in itself, guarantee an expansion in corporate power. They may signal the possibility of power, but deeper investigation is required before one can definitively establish that power is created by the interlocks or that power that is created is of any consequence. Further, the importance of interlocks varies significantly because of differences in power relationships within interlocking directorships. Thus, variation in the number of interlocks in no definitive way guarantees a change in the amount of power held by corporations. Accordingly, aggregating the number of corporate interlocks would provide an unreliable measure of corporate power.

After-Tax Corporate Profits as a Percentage of Personal or National Income

If corporations wield significant power in the aggregate economy, one would expect to see that reflected in their after-tax corporate profits. While after-tax corporate profits have increased over time, they have gradually declined as a percentage of both national and personal income. Does this mean that corporate power is waning? Not necessarily.

The corporate tax burden has declined as a share of total government revenue. While some of this is due to the lowering of corporate income tax rates, some can be explained by other changes in the tax laws. For example, corporations now are allowed to write-off depreciation at a faster pace and to use the last in-first out (LIFO) method of inventory valuation. This causes stated profits to be lower than they otherwise would have been. In other words, corporations may be just as profitable as before, but because of their ability to influence tax laws, they do not have to report as much of their profit.

"...corporations now are allowed to write-off depreciation at a faster pace..."

The decline in after-tax corporate profits may also be the consequence of well thought-out corporate policy. Galbraith, Dugger, and others support the assertion that corporations are willing to sacrifice short-term profits for power. To the extent that profits have actually fallen as a percentage of national and personal income, it may represent a willing sacrifice in order to gain and consolidate power.

After-tax corporate profits may have been adversely affected by foreign competition. In that case, one might infer that corporate power is declining. Alternatively, intensified foreign competition provides corporations with leverage in their efforts to freeze or cut wages. The result of intensified foreign competition may be that corporations more vigorously exercise their power in resource markets in an effort to maintain profits.

The Ratio of the Marginal Product of Labor to the Real Wage

In the neoclassical model, the marginal productivity theory of income distribution predicts that the real wage should equal the marginal product of labor. Gaps between real wages and labor productivity may result from imperfect competition and corporate power. If competition is imperfect, that is, if corporations wield power in the product and resource markets, we would expect the ratio of the marginal product of labor to the real wage to exceed one. By extension, the greater the gap between the marginal product and the real wage, the greater the degree of power exercised by firms.

Unfortunately, we lack a measure of the marginal product of labor and therefore cannot measure directly the ratio. However, if we assume constant returns to scale, then the average product of labor can be used in place of the marginal product. Inspection of the ratio of the average product to the real wage reveals that they are not equal and that the ratio is rising.

One limitation of this measure is that it focuses on the relationship between corporations and labor, and it ignores corporate interaction with government and other corporations. A second disadvantage of this measure is that it relies on the tenuous assumptions of the neoclassical model.

Percentage of Total Government Revenue Derived from Corporate Profits Taxes

Corporations, as well as the people they serve, have enhanced their own power and financial status, in part, through a multifaceted assault on government. This "capital-enhanced" minority, as Frederick Strobel calls them, has successfully influenced the "labor-dependent" to vote against their own interests, has "denigrated" government such that they have been coerced into cutting programs and reducing regulations, and has convinced enough policymakers that corporate tax cuts are in the nation's best interests. Promises of tax cuts and "trickle-down" economics persuade the "labor-dependent" to support policies that further the corporate agenda. Whatever the problem, the public is led to believe that government is to blame. The public mistrust of government helps further the corporate agenda as "anti-government"/"pro-business" candidates are ushered into office.

Measuring the percentage of total government revenue derived from corporate income taxes would potentially capture the more "political" efforts of corporations to further their own self-interests. Admittedly, the corporate "attack on government" is multifaceted, and no single measure is capable of doing justice to the wide and varied impacts of corporate activities. However, changes in the relative tax burden would seem to be a reasonable first indicator of the influence of corporations on government.

If corporate power is increasing, one would expect the corporate income tax share of total tax revenue to fall over time. From 1957 to 1991, the corporate income tax share fell from 18.3 percent to 7.1 percent. By contrast, the corporate share of total Gross Domestic Product remained relatively stable over the same time period. Thus, it would appear that while corporations have generated income at roughly the same pace as the rest of the economy, their share of the tax burden has declined. This would lend support to the conclusion that corporate influence over government policy has increased during the postwar period. It would also suggest that corporate income tax as a share of total tax revenue is an appropriate measure of corporate power.

Percentage of the Labor Force Unionized

Given the historical conflict between corporations and unions, it is reasonable to assert that successful corporate attacks on labor would lead to a decline in unionism. Reduced union membership would reduce the Galbraithian countervailing power that has helped to keep corporate power in check.

Union membership has declined steadily since the 1950s. Corporations, with the help of government (particularly during the 1980s), have undermined union effectiveness and made unions less attractive to potential members. At the same time, the elimination of traditionally unionized jobs in the manufacturing sector has weakened the core of union activity. Whether the decline in unionism is due to corporate machinations or other forces, corporate power is enhanced as labor's power wanes. To that extent, it is reasonable to treat the rate of unionization as a measure of corporate power.

Conclusion

This paper has provided an overview of some potentially effective measures of corporate power. Of those measures, the percentage of total government revenue derived from taxes on corporate profits and the percentage of the labor force unionized appear to hold the most promise. Practical and theoretical problems undermine the usefulness of the other measures, particularly if one is interested in empirically testing hypothesis using time series analysis.

For those heterodox economists attempting to operationalize hypotheses about corporate power, improvements in measures of corporate power are important steps.

Corporate Accountability[3]

10 Things You Know About Corporate Boards That Are Wrong

I'd like to thank Bill, and Bob especially for that excellent introduction. It was one of those good introductions that wraps up everything I'd want to spend 30 minutes saying in about 30 seconds. I'd also like to thank you for the honor of being invited here today to address the Economic Club of Detroit. This is acknowledged as one of the top 10 business speaking forums in the United States, and I consider it a privilege to speak with you.

Having said that, here I go insulting everyone in the room today with the topic of my speech, "10 Things You Know About Corporate Boards That Are Wrong." Because, even though this is a very business-savvy audience, I'm willing to bet that there are at least 10 things you know about boards of directors that are wrong, or incomplete, or outdated, or that bring unintended consequences in their wake.

Probably the first thing you know about boards that is wrong is that what you don't know about boards doesn't really matter. You know the score in business. Management manages, and the board is a group of old guys named George who get together every few months to drink coffee. They're not really a useful part of the business.

If you think this, I'll admit you have a lot of company. Several years ago, I interviewed business writer and speaker Tom Peters for my magazine. Tom Peters is a master at defining "excellence" and "wow" in business and I wanted to hear his tips for shaping an excellent, wow sort of boardroom. But after we talked for several minutes, I realized that Peters didn't have much to say on the topic. Now if you've ever seen one of Tom Peters' speeches live or on video, you know that his being at a loss for words is pretty newsworthy in itself, so I pressed him on the subject. He finally told me, "Look, when I was taking my MBA, I doubt we spent 30 seconds studying the board of directors." But he also told me that he now regrets this, because the board has started to truly matter.

And who else says the board of directors really "matters" today? Well, the Securities and Exchange Commission does. The SEC increasingly holds a company's board responsible for a firm's stock misdeed, for proper disclosure, and for audit irregularities. The major stock exchanges believe the board matters. More and more they mandate how the boards of listed companies are to be structured, and the makeup of their key commit-

[3] Speech delivered by Ralph D. Ward, publisher of *Boardroom Insider* newsletter and author, delivered to the Economic Club of Detroit, in Detroit, MI, on Mr 2 '98.

tees. Shareholders know that boards matter today. Annual meeting resolutions more often now focus on the board of directors, its independence, its pay, how it's elected, and its powers.

Most of all, corporate boards themselves now realize just how much they truly "matter." I can show this best here in the Motor City with an illustration. Suppose I were to travel back in time 10 years from today and visit you in your office. I try to impress you with all of the great world changes to come over the next decade, but you're a savvy businessperson, not easily impressed. I tell you that the Soviet Union—the Evil Empire—will, in short order, collapse on itself and that today Russia and what used to be its constituent republics are struggling to create their own capitalist systems. Well, you admit that is enormous news, historic in a global sense. But by 1988 you could see change coming, with Gorbachev already launching reforms, so you're not too shocked. Alright then, as a business person in Detroit, I hit you where you live. General Motors Corporation, the biggest corporation on earth. OK, now the BOARD of General Motors, you know, that group Ross Perot just derided as a panel of harmless pet rocks, nodding their heads when told. Well that GM board in 1992 will rise up to force the resignation of its own picked CEO and Chairman. Now wait, the fall of the Berlin Wall, you can deal with, but the GM board, launching a revolution? Now I have you at a loss for words.

"...it sounds like a golden age is dawning for corporate governance in America."

The GM boardroom coup of 1992 was followed over the next few months by more corporate boards rising up to sack under performing CEOs. IBM, American Express, Kodak, Westinghouse, and over the rest of the 1990's, other major firms, such as K-Mart. Apple Computer's board seemed to change its CEOs more often than it changed operating systems. And Apple also gave the ultimate proof that the board today matters in the health of a company. After its latest CEO firing last July, founder Steven Jobs came to the board and pointed out that, while CEOs had come and gone, results had continued to slip, and the real constant had been the Apple board. He convinced the board to restructure itself, adding more tech-savvy industry leaders. That's proof that the board matters, when it can accept itself as part of the problem.

This leads to something else we may know about boards that is wrong. Given that what I've just said is true, it sounds like a golden age is dawning for corporate governance in America. Boards will be wise and responsible, and sun will shine throughout the boardrooms of the world. In truth though, we may see just the opposite occur, and genuine crisis in our corporate boards, a crisis all the worse because it will afflict the very top of our corporate structure, just when we need them most.

The reason for this is that we are trying to create in the U.S. a model of corporate governance that has never really existed on a large scale here before. We want a board that is not the major owner of a company, that is not made up of the top managers.

We want directors who are independent outsiders yet are willing and able to assert solid, involved leadership and monitoring. And we don't know if that will really work.

One reason for this concern is what are called the "paradoxes" of the modern corporate board. We place much more responsibility and duties on our directors now, demanding much more of their time and effort; at the same time, all of us are facing far higher demands on our time and energy from our "day jobs," particularly the top executives who are the typical outside directors. We want boards that "look more like America," with more diversity, more women and minorities. We want more outside directors who are the star CEOs of our best performing corporations, who are still a largely pale male crew. We want directors to take a sharper interest in what's good for shareholders, keeping a close eye on building value, and having the courage to make major cuts or even sell the company when it will boost the stock price. We want our boards to use their status as the one body in a corporation with a long-term view to look out for the stakeholders, the employees, the communities, the greater public welfare. And while we're at it, we want to pay our boards to do all of these things at once.

That sure sounds like a crisis in the making. It suggests that we need changes in what boards do, how they operate, and how they structure themselves, Big Changes. A number of these Big Changes for reforming our boards have been advanced in recent years, most with major backing from shareholder activists. While I think many have good aspects, I've found that a lot of these Big Changes bring their own paradoxes, and end up being more things we think we know about the board that are wrong.

One of the best established Big Changes is that of splitting the offices of corporate chief executive officer and board chairman. In the United States, these positions are combined at probably three-quarters of our major corporations. The idea of one person holding both slots is so ingrained with us that we don't realize how unusual and uncommon it seems to the rest of the world. Step back and look at the idea: The CEO is the person in charge of management. The board chairman leads the body that oversees management. If the CEO and chair are the same person you get to grade your own report card. Writers and activists on governance issues have long advocated splitting the roles, and they saw their greatest success after the early-1990's boardroom coups I mentioned earlier. GM was the model here, with Jack Smith being named the new CEO of the automaker but board member John Smale holding on to the title of chairman to keep an eye on the turnaround. The "John and Jack Show" it was called in a New York Times article praising the setup. But in 1995, GM quietly ceded the chairman's position back to Jack Smith, and this pattern followed at the other coup companies as well. In California, the separate chairman idea is more common, with the board chair often representing the firm's capital sources, but even there, as the company grows and matures, the chairman's role tends to drift together with the CEO. Why is this? Remember that this is still the established model for most American business. Splitting the roles of CEO and chair at a corporation sends an unintended message to competitors, to markets, and within the company, that the CEO is a lame duck. This model may grow more popular in years to come, but I doubt it will become universal without a change in how we define the job of a separate board chairman.

Well, here's another idea. We want our directors to think like shareholders, so why not make sure they ARE shareholders? Why not pay members of the board in company stock. In fact, why not mandate that they should make their own investments in company stock out of their own pockets? This has been a very popular idea among shareholder activists. The National Association of Corporate Directors has made it a centerpiece of the several Blue Ribbon commissions they've held on setting governance standards. Al Dunlap, currently chairman of Sunbeam, is religious about this idea, and as soon as he joins a company, insists that his board members pay themselves wholly in stock, and that they dip into their own pockets to invest. But the mention of Al Dunlap hints at a possible problem with force-feeding directors on stock. Does it give the board short-term incentives to boost stock price? Does it also incent them to improve their liquidity by seeking to sell or break up the company, which should also give them a tidy premium? Finally does director stock pay and ownership really bring better results? The research is mixed.

"Major institutional shareholders own enormous chunks of equity in public companies."

The next Big Change is an extension of the above. Instead of trying to make our directors into being investors, why not turn our big investors into directors? Major institutional shareholders own enormous chunks of equity in public companies. CalPERS, which is the California public employees pension fund, is the single biggest public fund in the U.S. These pension funds have also been at the vanguard of pressing for governance reforms. Why not just put their representatives on the boards of companies they already own? Just this year we've seen a trend in this direction. CalPERS will soon vote on whether to nominate its own representatives to the boards of under performing companies.

The problem I've seen with funds going directly into the boardroom is that most of the fund people I talk to are loathe to take this step. The legal and fiduciary problems could be enormous. Suppose you are the fund representative on a corporate board. At a board meeting, you find out that trouble is brewing. Quarterly results will fall below analysts' expectations, or maybe a pending merger just fell through. The stock price will take a sharp hit. Now what do you do? Report back to the fund that it might be wise to unload? That's the perfect definition of "insider trading," and it won't do anyone any good for you to be led away in handcuffs. Do you sit tight though the dip in stock price? How soon will it be before one of your fund investors then sues YOU because you failed your fiduciary duty to them. You can build fire walls between what the fund's left hand knows and its right hand does, but liability dangers are still there waiting.

The final Big Change is the battle for board independence. Too few directors serve on too many boards, and too often they're tied into one another. If the CEO of company A serves on the board of company B and the CEO of company B is on the board of company A, won't these CEOs tend to "look out for each other?" The Walt Disney Company has made the covers of our major business journals in recent months. Just a couple of weeks ago, it was on the cover of Fortune as one of the 10 most admired companies in the United States. But a couple of months earlier, it made another top 10 list in Business Week—or bottom 10 list—among the U.S. companies with the worst boards. Disney is being hit for having a director with too many personal and business ties to CEO Michael Eisner. One director is principal at the school Eisner's children attended, and another was his personal financial adviser. At the Disney annual meeting last week, 35% of shareholders supported a resolution to restructure the board for greater independence.

What happens when we try to define board "independence" though? The IRS tried that several years ago when it passed legislation limiting CEO pay deductibility over $1 million unless CEO performance was reviewed by a board compensation committee of "independent" directors. The IRS draft definition roused an immediate firestorm though, because it was so tightly drawn that an outsider with virtually any business ties to the company would be ineligible. The IRS softened the rules, but this shows how hard it is to shape a usable, realistic definition of board independence. And as for Disney, its stock price has appreciated 43% over the past year; maybe more boards could use the CEO's kids' school principal as members!

Where does this leave us, then, with a pending crisis, but our Big Changes either untested, dubious, or bearing unintended consequences? If not Big Changes, how about little changes? Little, unsexy, administrative and human-scale reforms that could make our boards work better? Last fall, I launched an online newsletter called "Boardroom Insider" because it was just this sort of first-hand "how-to" that corporate directors really wanted to know about. They weren't asking me questions like "How do I shape our board to meet the demands of the 21st Century?" Instead they were asking things like "We have to cut our board meetings back from bimonthly to quarterly, how do we do more work in less time?" or "how can our directors digest the enormous amount of material they have to review?" or "two members of our board are always at each other's throats...how do we resolve this problem?" Reshaping how the board works, how it meets, and improving membership may sound small, but they are just the sort of fundamental, basic changes that can head off a governance crisis.

Start at the beginning, with board education, orientation, and continuing training. How many of you have served on a board? At the end of your first board meeting, wasn't there always at least one member who you looked at out of the corner of your eye and thought "How did that clown get here?" He doesn't know the company, he doesn't know procedures?" That shows how vital it is to improve board training, with review of the company, its markets, its competitors, its history, important contacts, and legal and regulatory issues. Follow this up with ongoing education on changes in the markets, in technology and potential liabilities.

Boards need to put more quality thinking into their scheduling and agenda setting. You have less time to meet, so use every minute of board and committee time most efficiently. Could you better schedule board meetings so quarterly financials would be both complete, and yet fresh? If you hold a board reception the night before the meeting, are you using this informal time for background discussion that can save board time the next day? Board work today is growing more technical, so this makes it more effective and efficient to do more in committees, which can specialize. Look over your committee charters to make sure they reflect this change, and allow the committees to work at their peak.

"Teleconferencing is today a popular board and committee meeting stopgap."

Speaking of charters, you DO have them for both the board and committees, and regularly review them, don't you? These charters will make it easier to institute one of the most powerful of board reforms, a board evaluation program. Set a schedule that assures board and committee evaluation at least yearly, and consider bringing in an outside facilitator to assist.

High tech is changing the way we all do business, but are you using it effectively in your boardroom? Are directors able to tap into your company nets to get the information and make the contacts they need? Teleconferencing is today a popular board and committee meeting stopgap. Why not build it into your committee charters? Suppose your audit committee held "face time" meetings only a couple of times per year, but conducted a scheduled 20 minute video-conference every month? What would the committee do with so much meeting time? A lot more than it does now.

As I said these are not sexy changes. No one will write them up in the Harvard Business Review, and consultants are unlikely to grow rich selling them. But they might just be the sort of "nuts and bolts" reforms that help us prevent a 21st century boardroom crisis. Thank you.

Mergers 'R Us: Has Antitrust Gone the Way of the 5 & 10?[4]

"Antitrust" conjures up heroic images from the past when big was bad. In 1902, Teddy Roosevelt charged into battle with railroad magnates James Pierpont Morgan and James J. Hill. In the 1940s, Franklin Roosevelt's antitrust chief, Thurman Arnold, busted the wartime world cartels commandeered by German industrialists. And in 1966, Supreme Court Justice William Douglas wrote that the concentration of economic power threatened our democracy, and that "control of American business [was] being transferred from local communities to distant cities where men on the 54th floor with only balance sheets and profit and loss statements before them decide the fate of communities with which they have little or no relationship."

"A nation of clerks," Douglas said, "is anathema to the American antitrust dream." Today, giant mergers mock the justice's words: Boeing combines with McDonnell Douglas; Sandoz with Ciba Geigy; British Telecom with MCI; Morgan Stanley with Dean Witter; B.A.T. with American Tobacco; Boston Scientific with Cardiovascular Imaging; Chemical Bank with Chase Manhattan, and Hilton Hotels pursues Sheraton/ITT. Yet Americans seem less concerned about being reduced to a nation of clerks than about being uncompetitive in foreign markets or being left unemployed by foreign competition. The fact is that antitrust law is not what it used to be; it was redefined in the early 1980s, at the start of the Reagan administration. Rather than being anti-bigness, antitrust law became pro-efficiency. In response to early winds of global competition, the law was cut back to its most minimal interpretation. Big businesses gained greater freedom to do what they wanted, and all businesses gained greater certainty about what they could and could not do.

Something has been lost of the old antitrust dream, which mirrored the pioneering spirit and ideals of Jeffersonian democracy. The vision was built on a populist distrust of power and large corporate size. As Senator John Sherman said in 1890: If we will not tolerate a monarch, we will not tolerate a king of trade. His legacy, the Sherman Act, reflected the idea that individual entrepreneurs should have autonomy and opportunity, that consumers should have sovereignty, and that entrepreneurs and consumers should be free from oppressive corporate power. It reflected an understanding that the dynamic interaction of all market forces would create an impersonal system of market governance, so that individual entrepreneurs and consumers would

---

[4] Article by Eleanor M. Fox, Walter J. Derenberg professor of trade regulation at New York University School of Law, from *The Washington Post* Mr 30 '97.

be ruled neither by public nor private power. Competition itself would assure economic and political democracy.

The dream was alive and well in the 1960s when antitrust and civil rights worked hand in hand to defend the underdog, helping to assure opportunity to the less well established. The problem with the dream was that it failed to take into account the tension between promoting a society of small and middle-sized players and promoting efficiency—and by the late '70s Americans began to care more about efficiency. They demonstrated this by voting for Reagan, who promised to "get government off the back of business." The costs of "civil rights" antitrust were becoming visible with the onslaught of competition from efficient foreign firms, such as Japanese and German steel, automobile and electronics makers, who were making inroads into American markets.

"...it is a crucial instrument both to empower people to compete and to establish markets..."

By the 1980s, with the lowering of world trade barriers, the costs were widely felt. IBM, for example, complained that it was shackled by the government antitrust case against it, just at a time when technology was changing the landscape of the market. The Reagan administration subsequently withdrew its case. Global competitiveness became the new Holy Grail—and not just in the United States. In 1993, when the member nations of the European Community adopted the Maastricht Treaty creating the European Union, competitiveness was explicitly stated as a goal for European business.

Though the quest for competitiveness has taken on a life of its own, antitrust is no anachronism. On the contrary, it is a crucial instrument both to empower people to compete and to establish markets, as nations are increasingly adopting the free enterprise system. Some 30 countries already have antitrust laws, and most newly industrializing and reindustrializing economies are adopting them. Post-communist countries such as Poland, Hungary and the Czech Republic are using antitrust laws to prevent newly privatized monopolies from barring entry to entrepreneurs and exploiting consumers.

In the United States, however, markets are well developed, and the role for the efficient antitrust of the '90s may seem small. While American law had originally promoted competition by preventing small companies from being fenced out of markets by economic might, the current antitrust paradigm promotes competition only as a way to achieve greater efficiency. It does not handicap even monopoly firms. Cartels, which are agreements among competitors aimed solely at eliminating competition (e.g. price fixing agreements), remain illegal, because these agreements are virtually always inefficient and harmful to consumers. But most mergers can be justified, even when they trample upon small and middle-sized firms. Even mergers of large U.S. firms may be procompetitive if the market is global and the combining firms face competition from strong foreign corporations. So mergers of major competitors, such as Boeing and McDonnell Douglas, may pass antitrust muster. If a merger threatens to reduce competition, the parties involved can usually make an agreement with the government enforcers for a minor spinoff of assets.

The facts are often different in markets that are local rather than global. This explains the recent actions of the Federal Trade Commission under the leadership of Robert Pitofsky. The FTC challenged the merger of the discount drug store chains Rite Aid and Revco; the companies abandoned the merger. Now the FTC seeks to halt Staples' acquisition of Office Depot—the two leading office supply discounting superstores—fearing that the combination would eliminate discounting and raise consumer prices. The FTC is studying whether a proposed sale of stores to the only other office supply superstore, Office Max, will cure the problem.

But an increasing amount of antitrust activity today is on the world stage. Transnational enforcement against world-wide price-fixing is strong. The antitrust agencies in the United States, Canada, the European Union and elsewhere work together to catch price fixers. Cooperation with Canadian authorities resulted in criminal antitrust enforcement against foreign firms charged with fax paper price-fixing and others charged with raising the price of plastic dinnerware for U.S. consumers. And cooperation with the European Union authorities resulted in decrees against Microsoft for its monopolistic practices on both sides of the Atlantic. U.S. antitrust enforcers James Rill, Anne Bingaman and Joel Klein—successive heads of the Antitrust Division of the Department of Justice—expanded U.S. vigilance against foreign firms that have exploited our citizens at home and excluded our exporters abroad. And the World Trade Organization has launched a new initiative to consider whether antitrust law should be internationalized to address world competition problems.

The use of antitrust to protect small and inefficient mom and pop stores is a luxury we can no longer afford. Today, the big challenge is whether we can protect the forces of global competition so Americans can reap benefits of dynamic markets—while the less rich countries and their people participate in them, too. The more daunting challenge is to do so while resisting two pulls: the nationalistic impulse to close our markets and keep out foreigners; and the impulse of the owners of capital to move their plants to locations that offer the lowest costs even at the expense of exploiting children, workers and environments, as symbolized by Nike's recent attraction to 20-cent child labor in Vietnam.

The shift in antitrust from protecting the weak against the powerful to helping even the powerful become efficient brings with it a responsibility to safeguard the values that footloose capitalism might destroy. Ironically, getting government off the backs of businesses as they engage in global competition should lead to regulations—international, if national will not work—to protect that still vibrant American dream: the autonomy and human rights of people.

The Good Side of Going Global[5]

It Opens the Gates to Growth

The industrial sites that are developing throughout the third world are often ugly and the wages they offer are low. Nevertheless, they symbolize a sea of change in the global economy, one which has the potential to raise the living standards of millions of people in today's poor countries.

This promise exists because we live in an era when advances in technology mean that, in Lester Thurow's words, "for the first time in human history, anything can be made anywhere and sold everywhere." Because this is the case, economic development has become a real possibility for all nations throughout the world. Globalization, in short, raises the possibility that, for the first time, the mass deprivation associated with underdevelopment might dramatically be reduced, if not eliminated. This liberating outcome will not happen automatically; globalization will have to be guided to make it as inclusive as possible. Nevertheless, it is realistic to believe that dramatic inroads can now be made against the scourges that afflict humankind in the third world: malnutrition, illness, and ignorance.

The surprise is that many liberals who identify with the poor have not seen globalization in this light. Indeed, on the political left globalization is seen as a process to be opposed and reversed if possible. Antipathy to globalization, for example, is prominent in the work of analysts at the Economic Policy Institute (EPI) such as Jeff Faux, Thea Lee, and Robert E. Scott. These authors argue against the growth in international trade which has been experienced in recent years as the result of globalization, and advocate neomercantilist, if not protectionist, trade policies for the United States. In the EPI's recent book, *Reclaiming Prosperity*, Scott is remarkably cavalier in asserting that most-favored-nation trading status may have to be withdrawn from Japan and from export-oriented developing countries, and that restrictions should be imposed on investment in specified developing nations. He betrays no anxiety at all that such policies could harm both the United States and the developing world by seriously disrupting international trade.

The EPI economists adopt this stance because they believe that U.S. imports of goods from poor countries and the flow of American capital to them have depressed wage rates in this country. In adopting this position they appeal to the work of Adrian Wood who argues that unskilled workers in developed countries have been hurt by globalization. But they cite Wood

---

[5] Article by Jay Mandle, professor of economics at Colgate University and coauthor, with Louis A. Ferleger, of *No Pain, No Gain* (A Twentieth Century Fund Paper). From *Commonweal* 124/13:11-13 Jl 18 '97. Copyright © 1997 *Commonweal*. Reprinted with permission.

only selectively. Ignored is what Wood says on the first page of his *North-South Trade, Employment, and Inequality* (Oxford, 1994): Trade "has had large benefits, raising average living standards in the North and accelerating development in the South." Ignored also is what Wood says concerning policies addressed to those hurt by the process: "The least attractive...policy response would be to raise barriers to imports from the South."

Globalization already has meant that numerous countries that formerly were considered to be "third-world nations" have become centers of modern production. South Korea, seen as an economic basket case in the 1960s, is only one of a number of Asian countries where economic growth, achieved by successfully penetrating export markets, has substantially raised the population's standard of living. To be sure, the spread of modern production has not really been global. Low-wage rates alone do not attract investment. A productive labor force, usually meaning a relatively well-educated population, is needed in most cases. So is reliable infrastructure: transportation, energy, and, of course, communications. But when these are present, rapid economic growth and therefore an escape from poverty become a very real possibility. The historic fact has been that such growth is the sole mechanism by which the living standards and well-being of large numbers of people have been advanced.

"...nations become increasingly important consumers and suppliers for each other."

The spread of economic modernization has long been associated with increased international trade. On one hand, development has permitted nations to export where previously they lacked the productive capacity to do so. On the other hand, growing incomes have permitted consumers to increase their purchases from overseas. With modernization, in the past as today, nations become increasingly important consumers and suppliers for each other. It is no surprise, therefore, that today U.S. trade with the rest of the world is growing. In just the last decade, our trade with the third-world countries of Asia, Africa, and Latin America has increased from 3.7 percent of the gross domestic product to 6.8 percent.

Trade-hostile liberals like the EPI analysts have not sufficiently considered the implications of their position for the growth of these underdeveloped countries. They are silent on the question of how, in the absence of trade, wages in poor countries could be increased over the long-run. Few on the left are willing to acknowledge what the historical experience of the developed world clearly demonstrates. The only realistic way labor incomes in poor countries can increase is by creating jobs which in the first instance are poorly paid. Higher incomes for working people need to be achieved, but this is possible only to the extent that productivity growth permits it. The antitrade liberals fail to acknowledge that curtailing access to the United States market would stifle that growth.

However, the globalization of trade promises not only to raise living standards in the poor nations. It also provides benefits to the people of developed nations such as the United States. This is because trade allows U.S. consumers to buy a wider array of goods and pay lower prices than would be the case if imports were barred or minimized. In effect, trade raises incomes by reducing prices, a consideration which was all but absent in the liberal opposition to NAFTA and appears not at all in the EPI studies of the impact of trade.

Those same low prices, it is true, do pose a threat to some U.S. industries. Generally these are industries that employ poorly skilled labor. Given the relatively high cost of labor in this country, goods produced with low-productivity workers, if traded internationally, tend to cost too much to be successful in world markets. The labor force in these industries therefore finds itself in competition with lower-cost workers in poor nations, a competition which puts downward pressure on wages and incomes.

However, curtailing trade as antitrade liberalism calls for is not a satisfactory answer to the problem of defining the role of a high-wage country like the United States in the globalized economy. Nor does it represent an adequate response to the situation of low-skilled/low-wage workers in this nation. Both of these problems require recognition of the fact that, to advance our society's well-being through international trade, we must specialize in industries in which we, despite our relatively high wages, nevertheless can be successful in the market place.

When labor-intensive production methods result in products becoming over-priced, we should engage in neither protectionism nor in a race to the bottom in wages. A better alternative would be to exit from those industries and specialize in the ones where we can be successful. In general, the latter will be those in which output per worker is high. This is because high levels of labor productivity can offset the cost effects of high wages. Exporting goods produced with high quality, highly paid labor would be a means to augment sales, thereby increasing the number of high-paying jobs in this country.

Adjusting the economy in this way requires that we do a much better job in ensuring that our working people possess the skills to be successful participants in the world economy. The widely acknowledged deficiencies in our educational system threaten our ability to create and sustain high-paying employment. Especially important in this regard is job retraining for workers who are displaced by technological advances and productivity growth. Such individuals retain the potential to be highly productive and should be helped to regain their place in a structure of production that can offer them high-wage employment.

The real danger lurking in the liberal antitrade position is that it concedes precisely what we have to fight for: a supportive government committed to advancing the productive skills of the labor force and offering an adequate safety net for those who confront difficulty in the highly competitive world economy. Instead, it turns to protectionism to provide jobs and raise incomes. Aside from the impossibly high price tag associated with such a strategy (one estimate has it that the cost of trade protection per job in the United States today is $170,000), this strategy turns its back on the legitimate interests of the poor in other, less-developed nations. Rather than pitting the poor of the developed world against the poor of the third world, as protectionism does, we should be prepared to continue to fight for economic justice everywhere. If the unskilled in this country need a public-sector jobs program because private-sector employment requirements exceed their capacity, that is what we should urge. If income transfers are required to assist the needy, that is what we should argue for. What we should not do is turn a blind eye to the needs of the poor elsewhere, something that is implicit in denying the developing world access to our markets.

"...the cost of trade protection per job in the United States today is $170,000..."

Obviously there should be limits to what is acceptable when the United States purchases goods from poor countries. We should not import goods produced by children or by workers who labor in demonstrably unsafe conditions. We should also ban the imports of products whose production processes contravene internationally negotiated environmental protections. But great care must be exercised in imposing such restrictions. The advocacy by Americans of trade sanctions to reshape labor and environmental policies in other countries risks a politically distasteful coercion. Our technological and environmental expertise should be made available where they are desired. The same is true with regard to our labor unions' assisting organizing efforts elsewhere. But such efforts must never represent impositions on unwilling societies.

Economic development in the third world is not the enemy of the well-being of the American people. Neither is the international trade associated with that development. But it is true that in today's international economy, in which low-income countries are emphasizing trade as the means to escape poverty, for U.S. workers to earn high and rising wages we will have to specialize in high productivity industries. Doing so requires an activist government, supportive of technological advance while at the same time compassionate about the human costs of that process. Better than we have in the past, we will have to reform our educational system to make certain that our workers can compete at the highest levels of productivity. At the same time we will have to recognize the interests and needs of those who are not successful participants in the process. In these ways, globalization can be harnessed to the task of extending the benefits of development internationally without dangerously pitting the people of the developed world against those of the third world.

II. The Corporate Presence

Editor's Introduction

Section II's goal is to portray the many facets of personal and public life into which the corporation has made a powerful foray. Corporate power is not merely a static concept reserved for Wall Street power plays, boardroom coups, or complex arrangements between firms. Nor is corporate power owed simply to corporations' creation of products upon which we have grown to depend. Corporate power, in its fullest sense, is the corporation's permeation into our everyday lives through a variety of subtle, often unnoticed means. A corporation's presence is enhanced by the constant barrage of advertising that interrupts television shows, covers buildings, and adorns the sides of buses. As we hum a corporate jingle, discuss a particularly catchy commercial, or pepper our language with slogans, we recall that corporation and thereby magnify its presence and its power.

This section begins by recalling the corporate presence as it is made known through advertising. The first article in this section discusses the proliferation of Tommy Hilfiger, both a popular brand of clothing and the name of the man responsible for a more than half-billion-dollar clothing empire. Currently, Tommy Hilfiger is one of the most recognized lines of clothing in the fashion industry. Hilfiger's advertising strategy is best described as all encompassing. According to the author, "It's impossible to walk down a street in America for any length of time before the red-white-and-blue Hilfiger name comes into view." Splashed not only on billboards, the Hilfiger name is often displayed in large, easy to read letters across the clothing itself. Thanks, in part, to this unprecedented level of visibility, the Hilfiger line appeals to multiple markets and subsequently generates staggering revenues. It also shows the power of advertising, both as a means of placing a product (and the corporation behind that product) into our vision and as a means of selling that product.

In the book excerpt titled "Let Them Eat Lifestyle," Tom Frank discusses the psychology of corporate advertising in which he believes "the world of business is the world, period." That is, corporations often tout their products as solutions that go beyond the minor difficulties such as cleaning clothes or finding inexpensive transportation. According to Frank, the modern-day corporation now bills products as able to solve deeper problems, which include individual identity, boredom, job frustration, etc. Frank terms such advertising "liberation marketing" and describes it as one of the central factors behind his belief that "The corporate takeover of life...has already happened."

Max Frankel in "Media Mongrels," discusses the invasion of advertising into a variety of previously unrelated media. The trend began with "advertorials," or advertisements masked as magazine articles. It continued in the infomercial, and has most recently landed on the Internet under the guise of Web sites that lure children with puzzles and games as a means of securing their personal information, which includes the brands they most often buy. Given this blurring of the line between commercial and content, advertising is, according to Frankel, a means by which the corporation enters our day-to-day lives often cloaked as something else.

The remaining articles in this section discuss the corporation's presence and power in arenas we might not expect. In addition to advertising, the corporation proliferates itself by purchasing (or taking it over) institutions, services, and places. Often that purchase is deemed a corporate intrusion and is subsequently resisted. Other times, however, the changes wrought by the corporation are clearly beneficial.

Peter T. Kilborn, in "Doctors Organize to Fight Corporate Intrusion," discusses corporate takeover in medical care and many doctors' resistance to it. According to Kilborn, health maintenance organizations and "investor-owned hospital corporations" are gradually assuming control of the health-care industry. The consequence is often a stress on efficiency and cost that, at times, conflicts with the doctor's obligation to the patient. Doctors subsequently become torn between their "oath to put the patient first" and their corporate performance bonuses.

Brian Doherty, writing for *Reason* magazine, discusses a subtle corporate presence, which is nonetheless having a very profound impact on the way art is produced, managed, and distributed. According to Doherty, the belief that corporate tactics will necessarily make art less pure is an outdated notion. Doherty profiles a variety of independent record label and comic book artists who have succeeded in "marry[ing] commercial interests with artistic integrity" by creating and managing their own companies to distribute their own art. Artists are thus utilizing the principles of corporate management much to their own profit. In this article, Doherty also profiles artists who have adopted corporate business practices without having signed themselves to a corporation. As this article demonstrates, the corporate presence is not only seen and heard, but is, in fact, a way of doing business.

Corporations have also made a well-publicized entrance into the world of professional sports. According to Roy S. Johnson, in "Take Me Out to the Boardroom," 52 major (public) corporations own "at least a slice" of a professional team, excluding football teams. The reaction to corporate ownership is mixed. On one level, corporations bring a measure of organization and efficiency that many leagues, particular baseball, desperately need. On another level, many fans fear that the age of corporate sports teams will turn a cherished institution into a series of business ventures. Whether or not dramatic changes ensue (and they very well may not), corporate-team ownership is yet another reminder of the corporation's power to buy and own what it sees as potentially profitable.

In a Word, Hilfiger: Fragrances, Film, Books on Fashion Titan's Runway[1]

The interview is over and Tommy Hilfiger is having his photo taken. He smiles his toothy Tommy Hilfiger smile, the flash pops over and over again, and then he remembers something.

"Hey, Craig, we didn't talk about Tommy," he yells out across the room. "No. 1 in the world now!"

Tommy is Hilfiger's cologne, just another rising star in the growing Hilfiger universe. The man behind the name, and the fragrance, didn't want it to be forgotten.

Hilfiger's not one to forget much. Beneath that boyish facade lurks a shrewd master marketer. How else could a word like Hilfiger become a household name?

Can Hilfiger, one of the hottest names of the '90s, get any hotter? The answer is yes.

Hilfiger's first megastore—complete with a Wolfgang Puck café—opens Sunday on Beverly Hills' Rodeo Drive. His first book, All American: A Style Book (Universe, $35), is in stores now, and a Hilfiger home line is coming next summer—everything from Hilfiger sheets and towels to Hilfiger furniture.

And on Super Bowl Sunday, a new fragrance, Hilfiger Athletics, will be launched along with his new athletic wear line in a 30-second TV commercial.

Forget Martha Stewart and her Kmart washcloths. It's the Tommy life everyone seems to clamor for now.

Hilfiger even hired the William Morris Agency this month to develop music, movie, TV and publishing projects.

All this, while Hilfiger's rank among the top 10 coolest brands with consumers ages 12-19 remains intact.

From the rough and tumble streets of south central Los Angeles to the halls of the Ivy League, Hilfiger is still the man.

Urban kids wear his clothes for the flashy designer cachet, and suburban kids wear his clothes to be as cool as the urban kids. Get it? It's a perfect circle for Hilfiger.

Then throw in Bill Clinton, Bill Bradley and Prince Charles as Hilfiger customers, and add a few million wives trying to spruce up their middle-age husbands' wardrobes with some jaunty, sporty Hilfiger duds, and you can see he's got the market nicely covered.

His clothes are so hip they're celebrated in rap songs, yet they're still welcome at the tennis club in Greenwich, Conn.,

---

[1] Article by Craig Wilson, from *USA Today*, N 12 '97.

where Hilfiger shares a $10 million estate with his wife and four children.

It's impossible to walk down a street in America for any length of time before the red-white-and-blue Hilfiger name comes into view. If it's not on a person, it's on a bus stop billboard.

Even for the 46-year-old Hilfiger, it seems unreal at times.

"I always thought I'd be successful," he says, "but not to this extent, or this quickly. At times it seems sort of like a miracle."

Men's sportswear sales at Hilfiger grew to more than $400 million by the end of its fiscal year last March, and total sales reached over $660 million. Hilfiger's new athletic shoes alone could bring in as much as $65 million the first year, according to industry watchers.

"Hilfiger's new athletic shoes alone could bring in as much as $65 million the first year..."

And people still flock to see him when he makes public appearances at department stores—something he admits he's more than a little perplexed by.

"(But) I think people like to meet the person behind the name, whether it's a musician, an artist, a chef or someone who designs clothes."

Is Hilfiger a clothing designer? There are some who say no. New York magazine last year asked if perhaps he was just a "stylist," not in the league of fashion big boys like Ralph Lauren and Calvin Klein. His critics say he just "translates, scrubs and repackages."

Hilfiger has long been seen as an upstart in the fashion industry. Despite being named Menswear Designer of the Year by the Council of Fashion Designers in 1995—an award that's fashion's equivalent to the Oscar—he's still looked down upon by fashion snobs as nothing more than a rag merchant.

Does he care?

"Not any longer," he says. "I used to. But we're all merchants. We're all business people and designers. The designer has to be a good business person today. I look at myself as having both attributes. The creative mind and the business mind."

A story from Hilfiger's early years in New York shows he has plenty of both. It explains why Hilfiger is splashed all over everything, why his name became one huge logo, why he became one huge success.

Hilfiger says when his clothing began being sold in department stores, retailers didn't want big signs with his name on them.

"So I thought I'd get around that by using my clothes as signage, he says. "And the minute we put those items on a mannequin—with the name splashed all over it—they flew off the shelf."

Hilfiger's theory is that they sold because they were unique. They keep selling now because they're worn by the right people.

They also have a twist, as Hilfiger likes to say. He loves using the word "twist."

He says his clothes are "traditional with a twist."

He says his new women's line is "traditional with a twist."

He says his new home line will be "traditional with a twist."

Everything he does is "with a twist."

And that, he says, is where he departs from Ralph Lauren, the man he's often compared to—frequently in a poor-cousin sort of way.

As for Lauren, Hilfiger says he greatly admires the American icon.

"But I'm not Ralph Lauren. My customer is much younger, much more spirited, alive, energetic. He wants something more unique. I'm dressing the musicians. The rap stars. That separates us. And when the rap star wears something from us, people pick up on it."

And there lies one of the keys to Hilfiger's success. He has been brilliant along these lines.

Early on he would have young hip-hop groups come to his memorabilia-filled office to chat, to find out what they wanted to wear, to see what they thought was cool.

"Invite 'em up!" became Hilfiger's directive to his staff.

And it worked. He dressed them up head to toe in oversize Hilfiger—everyone from Snoop Doggy Dogg to Dr. Dre—and sent them off, later reaping millions of dollars through sales of Hilfiger clothing to their fans.

He says he doesn't have to invite these street-smart rappers up to his office anymore; now he has 100 designers who are themselves hip and happening. They know what the word on the street is.

"We have surfers and skateboarders, Asians and Spanish and Chinese and gays and straights. They tell me what they like and don't like."

The multicultural chemistry of the Hilfiger corporation is one of its hallmarks. Even the company's mission statement (his employees have to go to Tommy University) says that "by respecting one another we can reach all cultures and communities."

That's what disturbed him so about the false rumor, circulated on the Internet a while back, that he was a racist who didn't want blacks and Asians wearing his clothes.

"We've always had great respect for what comes from the street.... The baggy, oversized look is now part of America's heritage," he says proudly.

Will there be a day, though, when the Hilfiger name will disappear from the American streetscape? Could be, and it might be sooner than you think. Hilfiger has already started making his logos smaller, stripping his name off some of the clothes altogether.

He says he wants to be on the forefront of this cleaner, less cluttered, logo-free look. He says he doesn't want to be caught in a logo rut.

The logos and outside branding will remain on the athletic and jeans wear, he says.

"But we have two kinds of customers," he says. "The younger ones do want the logos. Big ones!

"But the older ones don't want the logos. They want things more subtle, more traditional."

And Hilfiger, who bills himself as the man for all people, will make sure he gives them both exactly what they want.

Let Them Eat Lifestyle[2]

Anybody who watches TV these days knows about the earth-shattering cultural change that's underway. Those who are optimistic about this shift argue that once we all own high-capacity computers, society will become radically decentralized and the nightmares of authoritarian government and soulless mass society, along with the age-old curse of elitism, will be ended for good. But those who are less sanguine see the big change as essentially negative. The sky really is falling, they rail, and civilization is wandering into a cultural catastrophe.

In part, of course, this is a predictable end-of-the-century sentiment, common to every year cursed with a nine as its third digit. But it's also a very real constellation of fears. As a culture, we've lost the ability to tell what's important and what's trivial. And nothing brings it home more concretely than the rise of the "culture trust," the group of media-behemoths like Time Warner, Geffen, Disney, and Westinghouse that have fashioned an industrial entertainment monopoly. What's happening looks like an almost literal realization of previous generations' fears of a totalitarian mass society: ever fewer voices talking to an ever larger and an ever more passive audience.

Both cyber-ecstatics and doomsayers are talking about the same larger phenomenon: the so-called information revolution and the unparalleled rise of corporate power that it seems to be fueling. The defining fact of American life in the 1990s is its complete reorganization around the needs of corporations. The world of business, it seems, is becoming the world, period. The market is politics, the office is society, the brand is equivalent to human identity.

Fast Company, one of the most prominent new magazines of recent years, calls this "the business revolution" and argues that business culture is replacing civil society. "Work is personal" and "computing is social" are points one and two in *Fast Company*'s manifesto for the corporate revolution. If there's going to be any social justice in the world, the magazine contends, it will be because the market has decreed that there be social justice. One of the magazine's writers takes the argument all the way: "Corporations have become the dominant institution of our time," he writes, "occupying the position of the church of the Middle Ages and the nation-state of the past two centuries."

To many of us, this summons unpleasant images. It's going to be the triumph of hierarchy, of homogeneity, of spirit-killing order. Right? We're all going to be robots and automatons. We'll have to listen to Muzak all the time. It's going to be like 1984 or

---

[2] Book excerpt from *Conglomerates and the Media* (The New Press, 1997) by Thomas C. Frank, editor-in-chief of *The Baffler*, reprinted from *Utne Reader* (Nov.–Dec.) D '97. Copyright ©1997 The New Press. Reprinted with permission.

one of those dystopic Schwarzenegger films. Right?

Wrong. The corporate takeover of life in fact has already happened, but one of the most salient characteristics of our emerging corporocracy—this Republic of Business—is that it doesn't demand order, conformity, gray clothes, and Muzak; it presents itself as an opponent to those very things.

Business theory today is about revolution, not about status or hierarchy; it's about liberation, not order. Business is "fast companies" questioning everything from job duties to pay scales to office furniture. Business is thinking "outside the box," as anyone who has flipped through the latest management best-sellers must be tired of hearing. Business is tattooed executives snowboarding down K2 or shrieking down the halls of the great bureaucracies overturning desks and throwing paper. Business is adman Jay Chiat snipping off his clients' ties.

"Mainstream commercial America is in love with everything alternative..."

And all this makes for a peculiar national culture marked by a strange coexistence of, on the one hand, extreme political apathy and, on the other, extreme commercial extremism. Politically speaking, dissent against the market order has never been more negligible. In terms of politicians and political commentators, we are living in a time of greater consensus and conformity than the '50s. But take a look at our advertising. Mainstream commercial America is in love with everything alternative, way beyond anything we saw in the '60s. Even the word extreme itself is everywhere, from Taco Bell's "extreme value combos" to Boston Market's "extreme carver" sandwiches to commercials in which Pontiac announces that it is "taking it to the extreme." Not only can the center not hold; the canter ceased to hold about 30 years ago. And nobody cares. Certainly the traditional guardians of order don't care, and certainly the business community doesn't care.

Hip is how business understands itself today. And if we're ever going to challenge the power of the corporate culture, the first thing we're going to have to do is to understand that capitalism is different now, especially in the media and advertising industries.

If you talk about culture in this Republic of Business, sooner or later you have to talk about advertising, which remains the central ideological apparatus of the new capitalism. Advertising is the market's subsidizing mechanism, the free-enterprise version of the National Endowment for the Arts, the device through which creative talent is rewarded and cultural enterprises succeed or fail. Advertising is also the public face of capitalism, the device through which what Rutgers University history professor Jackson Lears calls the "fables of abundance" are transmitted and elaborated. The people who make advertising are, in a very real sense, the ideologues of the corporate revolution: They are architects of dissatisfaction and of perpetual obsolescence.

And though it's fun, and even vaguely empowering (to use the catchall adjective of our time) to talk about how oppressive and conformist consumer society is, if you look closely, you'll find advertising nodding in agreement. To be sure, here and there you will come across an ad depicting families whose happiness is consummated by products but, by and large, the work of the cutting-edge agencies is much hipper than that. Advertising, at least on its surface, does not regard the new world of total corporate control as a happy thing.

In fact, a lot of advertising today is full-on critical. It speaks directly to the problems of media, power, and culture. It makes exemplary use of all those images of people in the workplace as robots in uniform gray, trapped in box-like elevators and cubicles, driven by sadistic bosses. Advertising recognizes that consumer society hasn't given us the things it promised or solved the problems it was supposed to solve, that consumerism is in fact a gigantic sham. It's lots of hard work for no reason. The rat race. The treadmill. The office as hell.

Call this species of advertising "liberation marketing," to adapt a phrase from business guru Tom Peters. It knows that the culture trust exists, and it knows that business has conquered the world. And in response it offers not just soaps that get your whites whiter, but soaps that liberate you, soda pops that are emblems of individualism, and counter-hegemonic hamburgers. Liberation marketing takes the old critique of mass culture—consumerism as conformity—fully into account, acknowledges it, examines it, and resolves it. Liberation marketing imagines consumers breaking free from the old enforcers of order, tearing loose from the shackles with which capitalism bound us, escaping the routine of bureaucracy and hierarchy, getting in touch with our true selves, and, finally, finding authenticity, that holiest of consumer grails.

The roots of liberation marketing can be traced back to the 1960s, but its true debut was the famous 1984 TV commercial that introduced Apple's Macintosh computer, in which herds of people in gray were freed from the iron grip of Big Brother's propaganda telescreens. (Ironically, the announcement of Microsoft's "rescue" of Apple featured Bill Gates on a telescreen eerily similar to ones in that commercial.) The ad was remarkable not only for the way it was filmed and when it was shown (during the Super Bowl, of course), but for daring to accept, and even endorse, the darkest vision of consumer society. We are a nation of lookalike suckers, it told us, glued to the tube, fastening intently on the words of the Man. Until the Macintosh arrives, that is. The commercial set the tone not only for future Macintosh advertising, but also for the entire body of propaganda for the cyber-revolution that now deluges us every day: Computers are liberating; they empower us; they let us mouth off at authority.

Nowadays, you'll find liberation marketing everywhere—even in ads for chewing gum. Doublemint, for example, abandoned its happy jingle to tantalize us with a vision of the workplace as adult hell and its product as a glimmer of childlike innocence that we can enjoy surreptitiously anywhere. In the "Drivers Wanted" series of Volkswagen commercials, each installment identifies some aspect of consumer society which driving a Volkswagen enables you to resist: fakeness, overwork, boredom, compartmentalization, hierarchy. Especially moving is the spot that describes the soulless glass-and-steel office blocks, in which you are imprisoned.

One of the curious subtexts of liberation marketing is how often commercials are set in the workplace and how they mirror contemporary management philosophies favored by the sponsor, thc advertising agency, or the target audience. This is done explicitly in a French Macintosh ad: A rich Italian businessman explains to his son that workers are there to carry out orders and not to think. Otherwise, they'd want to change things, and this does not lie within the scope of their abilities. The voice-over comments: "There are different ways of running a company. Here's one." The Apple logo appears on the screen. The voice-over continues: "Luckily, there are others."

"...Microsoft celebrates a libertarian outlook by showing how it foils bureaucracy."

But this kind of anti-establishment approach would never work for the all-devouring Microsoft, which has to find some aspect of mass society other than the spectre of Big Brother to set itself against. Instead, Microsoft celebrates a libertarian outlook by showing how it foils bureaucracy.

Contemporary youth culture is liberation marketing's native tongue, but it will also scour history for long-dead emblems of hip, as in the Gap ads featuring Chet Baker, Montgomery Clift, and Jack Kerouac in khaki pants. Since the Beats are, apart from some of the early avant-garde artists, just about the earliest glimmering of the rebellion-through-style against mass society that defines liberation marketing, their works are a revered canon of contemporary advertising. In one Volvo commercial, the only spoken words are lines from Kerouac's *On the Road*. But it's important to Volvo that we understand that the ad campaign is true to the spirit of Kerouac, not just the image. The print ad reads: "Always the romantic, John remembered to bring *On the Road*. Not one of those new printings he'd seen in the bookstore at the mall, but the original one that he had stored away in the attic." Even advertising is down on mall culture! Find the authentic item in an attic somewhere, and hang it from the rearview mirror in your Volvo!

Here's the Kerouac passage in the commercial: "The only people for me are the mad ones, the ones who are mad to live, mad to talk, mad to be saved, desirous of everything at the same time, the ones who never yawn or say a commonplace thing." It's a virtual declaration of postmodern consumer desire: the hunger to consume everything at once, to defy the commonplace stuff that other people consume or that we consumed yesterday. It's a line that all copywriters should paste above their doors; a line that belongs in the Norton anthology of great consumer fantasies.

When I say this is an age of conformity on a level that far exceeds that of the '50s, I'm not saying there is no cultural dissidence in America. In fact, we have a superabundance of it. Even oldsters who drive the safe, sensible Volvo recognize that the "only ones" are the "mad ones." And look around at other aspects of the media: we are an immensely cynical people when it comes to the culture trust. Media workers, their bosses, and suits in general are stereotypical villains in contemporary mass culture. Nobody except Newt Gingrich likes Rupert Murdoch. We all know bad things are happening to our political and social universe; we know that business is colonizing ever larger chunks of American culture; and we know that advertising tells lies. We are all sick to death of the consumer culture. We all want to resist conformity. We all want to be our own dog.

And yet we do nothing.

I want to suggest that our apathy has a specific relationship to liberation marketing. The market works not only to redefine dissent, but also to occupy the niche that dissident voices used to occupy in the American cultural spectrum. There's an inverse relationship between the prevalence of advertising and America's political apathy. Marshall McLuhan pointed this out back in 1957 in an essay, "American Advertising," describing a letter written by an American army officer stationed in Italy after World War II: "[The officer] noted with misgiving that Italians could tell you the names of cabinet ministers but not the names of commodities preferred by Italian celebrities. Furthermore, the wall space of Italian cities was given over to political rather than commercial slogans. Finally, he predicted that there was small hope that Italians would ever achieve any sort of domestic prosperity or calm until they began to worry about the rival claims of cornflakes or cigarettes rather than the capacities of public men. In fact, he went so far as to say that democratic freedom very largely consists of ignoring politics and worrying about the means of defeating underarm odor, scaly scalp, hairy legs, dull complexion, unruly hair, borderline anemia, athlete's foot, and sluggish bowels."

The point I'm trying to make is not that advertising somehow tricks us into ignoring our problems, but that the culture of consumerism has undergone an enormous change. Dissidence has been channeled into the marketplace; existential rebellion is becoming just as powerful an element of brand loyalty as the 12 ways in which Wonder Bread built strong bodies ever were. When we talk about nonconformity, we're increasingly talking about those particularly outspoken entrepreneurs who are detailed in *Wired* magazine When we talk about breaking the rules, we're talking about the people who are in their offices all night but listen to alternative rock while they're there. This is a point that French advertising executive Jean-Marie Dru makes explicitly. Every brand must have an identity, he says, and the most effective identities are those that take on the trappings of social justice: "The great brands...have succeeded in conveying their vision by questioning certain conventions, whether it's Apple's humanist vision, which reverses the relationship between people and machines; Benetton's libertarian vision, which overthrows communication conventions; Microsoft's progressive vision, which topples bureaucratic barriers; or Virgin's anticonformist vision, which rebels against the powers that be." The Body Shop owns compassion, Nike spirituality, Pepsi and MTV youthful rebellion.

With its constant talk of liberation, the advertising industry is filling a very specific niche in the cultural spectrum of the Republic of Business. As business replaces civil society, advertising is taking over the cultural functions that used to be filled by the left. Dreaming of a better world is now the work of marketers. We used to have movements for change; now we have products. As American politics become ever more deaf to the idea that the market might not be the best solution for every social problem, the market, bless its invisible heart, is seeing to it that the duties of the left do not go unfilled.

If capitalism's only problems were soul-deadening conformity and lack of authenticity, then it could solve them very effectively—as it has been since the 1960s. But if your idea of capitalism's problems swings more heavily toward sweatshops and downsizing and union busting, then you're talking about something else altogether. This is a critique that advertising will never embrace. No matter how hard up Reebok gets, it will never use the fact of Nike's Indonesian sweatshops to improve its market position. No, it'll just keep talking about how its shoes let U.B.U.

Advertising has real trouble solving concrete social problems. Not that it doesn't try. Get-rich-quick schemes are being sold as solutions to unemployment in a recent spate of ads. And then there's the famous Pizza Hut commercial in which management has pizzas delivered to a picket line. The strikers drop their signs, grab a slice, and look up gratefully at the benevolent boss' office window. Problem solved.

So we're back to where we started: The world of business is the world, period. There's nothing outside of it; it's a closed universe. Get as mad as you want. Just be sure the pizza trucks are standing by.

Media Mongrels[3]

I once ordered a sheriff's badge with a coupon snatched from the back of a cereal box. When Mom didn't yank those boxes off the table, they also enthralled me with offers of magic wands and club kerchiefs. Although my orders were to buy cereals strictly for the taste of the stuff inside, I feigned enthusiasm even for shredded wheat just to savor the prizes pitched on the outside. In short, I grew up expecting content and commerce to work in symbiotic harmony, like the articles and advertisements in a newspaper, or comedies and commercials on television.

Despite their coexistence, however, content and commerce always struck me as yin and yang, clearly distinguishable from each other. So I'm distressed to find the distinction being progressively blurred. An entire industry has arisen to confuse the two by breeding media mongrels. It is starting to relish the anarchy of the Internet, aiming abusively at young children, who are touted as a "lucrative cybertot category" of advertising.

The blurring began modestly enough with the invention of "advertorials"—magazine ads that masquerade as editorial content. Advertorials mix advertisements with inoffensive prose. An advertorial in this magazine last January, for example, packaged the ads of New York hotels with a George Plimpton essay celebrating New York's cultural attractions. The hotels were thus assured that their ads would not land beside a discussion of urban crime or Broadway flops. The *Times* takes some care to police these hybrids. Plimpton's prose was plainly labeled "advertisement" and set in a distinctive typeface. Other publishers, however, neglect such safeguards and often help the creators of advertorials to mislead their readers.

A decade ago, after the Government removed its time restraints on broadcast advertising, the mongrelizing came to television in the form of half-hour "infomercials"—commercials that masquerade as information programs. They present happy hawkers and gushing celebrities pitching facial creams and Magic Mops, hip reducers and slicer-dicers. Infomercials have also been adapted to the marketing of eccentric political products, like Steve Forbes and Ross Perot.

Predictably, their success led to the formation of a National Infomercial Marketing Association, wherein the half-hour hucksters align themselves with the round-the-clock marketeers of home shopping networks. The association now draws thousands of practitioners and performers to its conventions and bestows annual awards for noteworthy achievement. The most successful

---

[3] Article by Max Frankel, from *New York Times Magazine* p20-1 Je 2 '96.

recent infomercial is said to be the "Psychic Friends Network," on which celebrities like Dionne Warwick urge listeners to have their fortunes told by telephone, at $3.99 a minute. Last year's big hit was "Making Love Work," which featured Barbara De Angelis applying the experience of her five marriages to the sale of tapes and books that promise a happy relationship.

Young children, fortunately, have been insulated from these television lures by rules and circumstance. Rising ad rates are forcing infomercials to concentrate on expensive products like abdominal flexers and bust expanders. Also, children's programs remain subject to special scrutiny by the Federal Trade Commission. Though artfully tied to promotions for toys and T-shirts, the kids' cartoons are still required to separate content from commercials, to limit the time allotted to advertising and to avoid sales pitches by trusted on-air hosts.

No such restraints apply on the Internet, where dozens of familiar companies aim to lure even preschool kids with puzzles and prizes and "personal messages" from the Nabisco Thing, the Colgate Tooth Wizard and my old friends, the Kellogg triumvirate of Snap! Crackle! and Pop!

More cunning still are Web sites like "KidsCom—a Communications Playground Just for Kids, Ages 4 to 15." To play, I had only to give my name and computer address, age, sex, hobbies and family size and to reveal my life's ambition—"pick as many as you want"—from pilot to President. To earn KidsKash for redemption in the Loot Locker, I then had to tell what athletic shoes I wear, why I chose that brand, who paid for them and what kind of store I patronize. And I'll get more Kash if I enroll friends, parents and teachers, any 35 of whom would entitle me to a case of Nabisco cookies.

This "playground"—obviously more than a cereal-box diversion—belongs to SpectraCom, which calls itself "a strategic planning, interactive on-line marketing, research and communications company." It boasts of using KidsCom to pry into the lives of consumers so that their profiles can be sold to product merchants.

The new world of webmarts has been surveyed by the Center for Media Education, a children's lobby, and it has aroused the F.T.C. to begin this week to look into two worrisome trends. One points toward the creation of personalized ads aimed at individual children, with information pried from them on the Internet and from the furtive tracking of their on-line behavior. The other is the creation of computer environments that will capture children's attention for long periods with seamlessly integrated information and advertising, the kind of marketing that by consensus has been kept off children's television so far.

The center says psychologists have taught advertisers that young children are especially trusting of computer characters who address them by name and engage them in one-to-one conversation. The industry's research shows also that when children go on line they enter a "flow state" of total absorption in a challenging activity. Erica Gruen, of Saatchi & Saatchi Interactive. is quoted as certain that "there is nothing else that exists like it for advertisers to build relationships with kids."

I guess Mom was wrong to wean me off cereal boxes prematurely. It's never too early to prepare a child for the American way of commerce. With just a few more coupon cutouts, I might have grown up enjoying advertorials, infatuated with infomercials and wild about kidpitch on the Web.

Doctors Organize to Fight Corporate Intrusion[4]

In the first large organized backlash against what they call the industrialization of medicine, many doctors of Massachusetts' renowned medical schools and teaching hospitals are calling for a moratorium on corporate takeovers of health services and for curbs on the companies' intrusion into doctors' decision-making.

"It's time to put a stop to it," said Dr. Bernard Lown, 76, who, as chairman of the Ad Hoc Committee to Defend Health Care, is organizing the campaign.

"We are troubled by any organization that places an interface between the patient and the doctor," said Dr. Lown, a cardiologist and Harvard professor who shared a Nobel Peace Prize for organizing physicians against nuclear war.

For a couple of years, many of the nation's once-independent, self-employed doctors have been agitating against the proliferating managed care organizations that they see as jeopardizing their authority, jobs, income and patient care. A few thousand doctors, mostly in California and Florida, have joined unions to challenge the organizations.

But this is the first effort by doctors to call for changes in the practices of the managed care groups. It comes as consumer groups and state governments across the nation are pushing for new laws to weaken the power of health maintenance organizations with tougher regulatory control. And it is occurring in one of the nation's leading centers of hospitals and medical education.

By the middle of June, said Dr. Susan E. Bennett, 50, a primary-care physician and a campaign organizer, 1,940 Massachusetts doctors, young and old, men and women, liberal and conservative, most with ties to Harvard, had signed the committee's "Call to Action."

In view of the Clinton Administration's unsuccessful effort to overhaul the health care system three years ago, Dr. Bennett said, "We want to start a new national dialogue."

The Massachusetts doctors' appeal offers no alternative to the current health care system, but the doctors' dismay at its condition is stated in stark terms.

"Mounting shadows darken our calling and threaten to transform healing from a covenant into a business contract," the petition says in its opening paragraph.

Businesslike efficiency is essential to health care these days, it acknowledges, but not to the extent that it compromises the doctor's oath to put the patient first.

---

[4] Article by Peter T. Kilborn, from the *New York Times*, Jl 1 '97 p12.

The call, listing the names of the doctors who signed it, is scheduled to be published in the October issue of The Journal of the American Medical Association. Other doctors will then be invited to join. On July 10, the 22 doctors who make up the ad hoc committee, plan a nationwide telephone conference call to explain their campaign to doctors in other states.

Nearly two-thirds of the 188 graduates of the Harvard Medical School this month voted to support the campaign. The Massachusetts Medical Society, the mainstream group that represents most of the state's doctors, is forming a study group that is likely to propose statewide regulatory standards to assure that doctors can provide the care they deem best for their patients.

"We're mobilized," said Dr. Allan Goroll, president of the society, who is an internist at Massachusetts General Hospital and an associate professor at Harvard. "We support Dr. Lown's advocacy because it's advocacy for the preservation of the doctor-patient relationship."

"...many doctors say they have come under relentless pressure to subordinate patients' interests..."

As H.M.O.'s, insurance companies, hospitals and the nation's employers strive to hold down the costs, they have turned to lower-paid nurse-practitioners and physicians' assistants to provide more of the care, second-guessed the medications doctors prescribe and had patients get tests out of town where fees are lower.

In Massachusetts, 14 health maintenance organizations cover 45 percent of the population, one of the highest rates of any state, and in surveys, consumers rank some H.M.O.'s among the nation's best. But with a surge of consolidation of hospitals and health services in the past two years, and the recent arrival of investor-owned hospital corporations in the state, many doctors say they have come under relentless pressure to subordinate patients' interests to those of accountants and stockholders.

Dr. John D. Stoeckle, 74, the senior member of a 14-doctor primary-care group at Massachusetts General Hospital, is a case of a doctor grappling with all the changes, and not happily.

With the onset of managed care, the hospital began measuring the productivity of its doctors—the number of patients they saw in relation to the number they and the hospital set as their goal. If the doctors surpass their goal, they receive annual bonuses, and if they do not, their pay is cut. Dr. Stoeckle sees among the highest number of patients in the primary-care group—2,202 this year, through May—and surpassed his five-month goal of 1,562 by the highest proportion of any doctor in the group.

Yet, Dr. Stoeckle says, he will not rush. He starts seeing patients at 7A.M. "I'm not operating in the industrial world where a guy comes in for 15 minutes once a year," he said.

But Dr. Stoeckle is a member of the ad hoc committee. One reason, he says, is that he hopes a new national debate will lead to a system assuring health care for all. But another is managed care's intrusion of paperwork and bureaucratic second-guessing.

"It seemed more pragmatic," Dr. Stoeckle said. "But it's always cost, cost, cost."

Managed-care organizations maintain that they have arrested the once-soaring cost of health care, have raised the quality of care by tracking doctors' success in treating patients against national norms and have turned the focus of medicine from treating disease to preventing it. More efficient medicine, they add, has led to surpluses of hospital beds and specialist physicians and thus to the self-serving recrimination of doctors.

"I certainly recognize and live with some of the flaws and some of the value issues," said Dr. Joseph L. Dorsey, corporate medical director of Harvard Pilgrim Health Care, the state's biggest health maintenance organization. "But I don't believe society isn't served by good H.M.O.'s.

"Those in the feeding line are extremely angry. We are willing to be in the middle and strike the right balance."

Robert Hughes, president of the Massachusetts Association of H.M.O.'s, said the "Call to Action" was concentrated among liberal doctors with a political agenda and "age-old critics in the medical establishment."

Their anger over profit-making is misplaced, Mr. Hughes said, because any health care service, even a doctor's private practice, must receive more in revenue than it spends to stay in business.

"Even a church has to make a profit," he said.

Some doctors acknowledge that the excesses of their profession had helped bring about managed care.

"We don't want to go back to the days of doctors ripping off patients," said Dr. Jerry Avorn, a geriatrician and Harvard professor and one of the campaign's leaders. "Unless we acknowledge that, we're not going to be taken seriously."

Many other doctors have come to terms with the changes in practice with little complaint, including a colleague of Dr. Stoeckle, Dr. Larry Ronan, who declined to sign the "Call." Some management review of his care is better than working without any oversight, Dr. Ronan said, adding, "I welcome the education."

But Dr. Ronan, too, draws a line against efforts by managed care to reverse his decisions in patient care and deny patients the tests and procedures he deems necessary.

"I want to be able to do the kind of care I want for you and give you as much freedom as possible to choose," he said. "You can't take care of that patient unless that patient trusts you."

Among the Harvard Medical School's newest graduates, Dr. Jonathan Winickoff, 27, said that with his new medical degree and plans to become a pediatrician, he wondered what managed care meant for him.

"The reason you go into medicine is to alleviate suffering and make a difference in patients' lives," Dr. Winickoff said. "H.M.O.'s do some things that help," like providing feedback on doctors' performance and imposing quality controls.

"And they do some things that don't," he said, "like restrictions on tests and having to see 20 patients in half a day."

A classmate, Dr. Ann Hallward, 32, just beginning her internship in psychiatry, shares Dr. Winickoff's idealism. "The opportunity to help someone when they're vulnerable—that's a wonderful thing to be able to do with your life," Dr. Hallward said.

Dr. Hallward said managed care might have one noteworthy virtue. "If getting rich is not an incentive to enter medicine," she said, "if medicine attracts a different group of people, I think that's good."

The Embarrassment of Riches[5]

At the San Diego Comic Convention, an artist-rebel harangues a crowd of hundreds in a huge double hall in the convention center. His name is Todd McFarlane, and he is one of the most popular comic book artists of his generation. In 1992, he abandoned a safe berth with a giant entertainment corporation, Marvel Comics. McFarlane's art sold millions of Spider-Man comic books, and made him a wealthy man.

An insurrectionist and troublemaker, McFarlane enticed some of Marvel's other star attractions to quit with him, and set up a new umbrella company for their work: Image Comics. Image differs from big, traditional comic companies. The artists retain full ownership of their own characters and work. The business end of the company works for *them*, merely helping them with printing, promotion, and distribution. The creators are the bosses. In a field dominated for decades by two big companies—Marvel and DC (a subsidiary of Time Warner, the world's biggest entertainment conglomerate)—this was a truly revolutionary move: the independent creator at war with the big corporation.

Addressing the comics convention, McFarlane looks the part of the scruffy modern Bohemian, wearing a loose blue T-shirt, denim shorts, a dirty baseball cap, and a goatee. But as he swaggers and jokes, he seems to revel in demolishing some traditional preconceptions about the relationship between money and art.

Oh, money isn't important to him, this rich man assures the crowd, in the classic tradition of the artist rising above mundane concerns. Then the punchline: "The only good thing about money is, it you have enough of it, you can do whatever you want."

And he's doing it. Instead of licensing his popular superhero Spawn to some toy company, he started his own toy company. Sure, he's letting outsiders make movies and cartoons of Spawn, but he's keeping a close eye on them. He sounds like the traditional artist bashing corporations when he gleefully sneers that "the big corporations are bloated and fat. They can't catch a skinny little weasel like me." But then he makes a joke of the old cliche that to an artist, selling your creations for others to use and profit from is as bad as selling your children. "When I sell my kids," McFarlane jokes about his TV and movie deals, "I want visitation rights and some say in how they are raised."

Across the country, in another area of youth-oriented pop culture, Patrick Hughes tells another story of working outside the traditional corporate structure. Hughes runs an independent

---

5 Article by Brian Doherty, assistant editor of *Reason* and operator of Cherry Smash Records, a small independent record label, from *Reason* Ag/S '97.

record store, carrying only small-label independent releases, in Gainesville, Florida.

"I got a call from these guys who had just put out a record by a local band," he recalls. "It was their first time doing this, so they had some questions about the business end of it all. They wanted to know things about distribution, standard prices, and such. I gave them some advice about how to price it in line with the usual market rate, which would allow them to make their money back plus some.

"That stopped them. 'Oh, we don't want to make any money on it,' they told me. 'You know, it just wouldn't be right, it would just feel weird.' I couldn't really pin them down to *why* they felt this way. I mean, what's the problem? Charge an extra 50 cents, sell a couple hundred, use it as seed money to make another record, to pay postage on mailing it to radio stations around the country so more people can hear it.

"They said, 'I guess that might be cool and all, but we really don't wanna get into that sort of thing.' But what if you don't sell them all, I asked, don't you want a chance at making enough money off the ones you do sell to break even? 'Oh, we don't want to make money,' they said. 'We just wanna get this music out.'

"I tried to explain, you can get the music out more efficiently, make it go farther, have money to put out more music on a later date, by charging enough to make a sensible little profit. The whole notion that they could make a minimal amount of profit to plow back in was distasteful to them, like it would sully the purity of what they were doing."

"Increasingly, 'indie' artists have the chance to marry commercial interests with artistic integrity..."

The idea that commerce will necessarily "sully the purity" of art is a hoary one, common not only in the highbrow arts that rely on government and foundation grants but in the underground popular arts fed by fan enthusiasm. As one man who works in the distribution of independent records puts it, Nobody [in the independently produced arts] actually talks about the money because it's considered to be a very insincere source of inspiration, a dirty facet of a dirty business." While its sources are understandable, this attitude hurts artists, depriving them of both audiences and profits, and it helps infect the general culture with the sense that markets by their nature subvert important values.

As Hughes's and McFarlane's more balanced approaches suggest, however, something is changing. Increasingly, "indie" artists have the chance to marry commercial interests with artistic integrity—to get their art to more people without sacrificing their vision and, if they're lucky, to make even more money than they might by "selling out" to a big corporation. Entrepreneurship has become a real option for such artists, making trade not a vehicle for corruption but a way to communicate with fans.

Before the late 1970s, this was almost unheard of. Then, in the '80s, whole new ways of doing business arose in comics and rock, allowing artists to retain more control and ownership of their work. In both fields, new distribution networks and trade/commentary magazines developed to help sell and publicize these works, which appeal to a more limited audience than mass-market comics and rock. New technologies, such as desktop publishing and relatively inexpensive digital recording and manufacturing technologies, reduced the capital needed to enter the comics or record business. Today, starting a record company or publishing a comic book takes less capital than buying a five-year-old Honda Accord.

Some "indie" companies are just small, while others are actually run by the artists themselves. Either way, they're distinguished by their independence from big corporations. The large, traditional companies tend to take a more authoritarian hand in running artists' careers; retain ownership of all the characters and music; take a larger slice of any income; and are generally more bureaucratic. The deal they offer artists isn't all bad, of course. Big publishers and record companies also take care of key business details that can be as important to getting the work out as actually drawing the comics or playing the music.

Colleen Doran, creator of the formerly self-published comic book *A Distant Soil,* learned this lesson the hard way. Although she had publicly celebrated her independence from corporate paymasters, she relented last year, moving her comic book over to Image. Self-publishing, despite the freedom, has its downside, Doran explained to *The Comics Journal*: "You just don't have any clout when you're all by yourself....You can't negotiate, you can't get the best prices on printing...because you're just a single person. Your printer knows it, your distributor knows it....You just don't have any power."

Although Doran still owns her characters with Image, some of her fans did not approve of that compromise. In much of the in die world, self-publishing itself has become tied up in the "commerce sullies art" mentality. From the reaction of a vocal group of self-publishing acolytes, "You would have thought I'd raped someone's grandmother," she says. "The fans now perceive that self-publishing...is more important than our role as creators and the creation itself."

Self-publishing is "something of the '90s fad movement thing for hip creators to do," another former self-publisher, Matt Wagner, told *The Comics Journal*. To audiences used to consuming less-obscure portions of popular culture—television, movies, books—this whole issue might seem senseless. Who cares who sells or owns the cultural products you want? Besides, artistic self-production is almost unknown in other areas of pop culture, and is often considered disreputable.

In fact, when comic book artist Paul Pope began self-publishing in 1991, he created a phony persona to be his publisher. "My understanding was that self-publishing had this vanity stigma, and I wanted to avoid that," Pope says. "But when I started meeting other people in the comic business, I realized I was wrong. Literary self-publishing and comic self-publishing are perceived very differently." Not only is it not an embarrassment, there's an audience that considers it a definite plus. (Pope self-publishes his *THB* and also works for bigger companies, including the Japanese mega-publisher Kodansha.)

"Indieness" can be its own marketing tool. In the record field, many big labels create new subsidiaries to try to seem indie, emulating cheap-looking ad and promotion techniques that indies use out of financial necessity. (This same phenomenon can be seen now in the beer industry as well, where big breweries create new names to emulate hip microbrews.) And the small-press and self-published end of the comic market has been slowly gaining a larger market share—although that share is still small (about 5–10 percent)—of a rapidly collapsing market. (That share excludes Image, since its size and mostly superhero focus make it a slightly different animal, even though its characters are creator-owned. Even market leader *Spawn* has gone from a 1993 high of sales over a million copies to sales today of 160,000.)

Jeff Mason, who publishes *Indy*, a magazine dedicated to the world of self-published and small-press comics, explains the attraction: "It's very important to own your own thoughts. Selling your thoughts or signing away the rights to your thoughts is anathema. The idea that you can create something and it's not yours at all is bad. I want to give support to folks that are doing their own thing. If you don't own it yourself, you are at the whim of the person paying you. You aren't free to do what you want, you can't take risks, you can't create. Companies like Marvel and DC are like committees, and you can't create by committee. Committees don't tell stories, they just make demands." His magazine focuses not just on self-published comics but on any creator-owned comic.

Mason has a point—and provides insight into one reason why these audiences of pop culture cognoscenti fret over issues of ownership and corporate control. The world of small comics has delights to the discerning fan that one more fist fight between Spider-Man and Dr. Octopus just can't offer. The recent wave of deeply personal naturalistic autobiography in small comics—one of my favorite trends—isn't the sort of fare that adolescent-power-fantasy–oriented big companies provide. And Dave Sim's *Cerebus*, a self-publishing pioneer started in 1977, is doing something no big company has done: presenting a unified 300-issue-long narrative telling the entire life story of one character (a talking aardvark embroiled in the political and religious struggles of a mythical pre-industrial world), written and drawn by the same creator throughout.

But Sim is getting more out of self-publishing than creative freedom. Sometimes artists can have it all: integrity, freedom, and filthy lucre. Sim, for example, takes only $40,000 a year in salary from his company, but it owns a home for him to work out of, has no debt, and grosses half a million dollars a year. (Sim won't specify the net, but says it's "considerably" less.) His lack of debt, Sim says, "puts us well ahead of Time Warner, in my view." All this from selling his comic book to a monthly audience that has never topped 30,000 and now hovers around 12,000. The real money comes from repackaging his old comic books in large book collections. Sim is able to make sure that his entire life's work is always in print and always generating income for him. Even small niche markets can be lucrative when the creator controls *all* of the income stream (minus the distributors' and merchants' shares).

"Even small niche markets can be lucrative when the creator controls all of the income stream..."

Sim, to his credit, has never played the traditional "artists should starve in a garret for their art" role. He is known in the industry for his extravagant spending on travel and entertainment. *A Comics Journal* editorial once referred to him as "a man...who stays at the Savoy in London and serves his guests Beluga caviar while making pronouncements on such subjects as the greed of publishers." He regularly runs photos of himself in exotic vacation spots on the back cover of *Cerebus*.

Through much of 1995, Sim devoted both cover space—unheard of in a commercial comic—and long text pages at the front of his comic to advertising for the "Spirits of Independence" tour, a series of local conventions promoting independent creators and heralding the advantages and growing popularity of self-publishing among comic artists. He emphasizes the importance of maintaining control over how much of your work stays in print and available for sale. Even the large cash advances big companies can provide, Sim suggests, can pale in relation to the constant and long-lasting income stream total ownership of your work can provide.

Sometime self-publisher, sometime corporate employee Paul Pope agrees. He does see an aesthetic distinction between the comics he self-publishes and the work he does for bigger companies. "I put the more meaningful stuff out myself, the stuff that's important to me on a philosophical level as well as financial—the stuff I'm willing to take a 100 percent risk on. And with any investment, you're going to want to be able to get returns over time. The saving grace of self-publishing is that the decision about how long something stays in print and earning money is mine."

This is a lesson learned, in the underground rock field, by Mark Robinson, formerly of the band Unrest. Robinson has run his own label, Teen Beat Records, out of Arlington, Virginia, for 12 years. His band Unrest achieved popularity beyond his label's capacities—Robinson thought it too difficult to get the money together up front to pay for the recording and manufacturing costs that Unrest demanded. So he and the band signed first with a subsidiary of Virgin Records in the late '80s and then with a subsidiary of Time Warner in the early '90s.

Robinson ended up dissatisfied with the level of creative control over packaging he got from the Time Warner subsidiary—less than he was promised—and thought that in some cases he could have sold as many copies on his own as the bigger companies did. Now he doesn't own the music and has no say over keeping it in print. If he still controlled all of Unrest's records, Robinson says, he could still be making money off of them and attracting more wholesaler attention to his small label by offering the desired Unrest albums. (The rights to the Virgin subsidiary's records revert to Robinson after 10 years, though the ones with the Time Warner subsidiary are gone forever, he says.)

Robinson's dilemma limns a mostly unspoken truth about the indie ethos: "Selling out" can sometimes be less lucrative than the integrity of independence. This is especially true for the two most quoted avatars of independence from the corporate machine in rock, Ian MacKaye of the punk band Fugazi and Washington, D.C.'s Dischord Records, and Ani DiFranco, modern folk/punk troubadour.

If the Sex Pistols showed would-be punk kids that anyone could be a rock musician, MacKaye holds a similar place of honor in punk history for showing them that they could also control the production and sales of their own records. Looking over Fugazi's press clips, one finds MacKaye talking about "people who are into doing this music for life, not making any money out of it, but doing it because they have to" and how his label's goal was "not to make money, but to help as many of our friends' bands as we could." Fugazi has been the loudest and most steadfast holdout—especially in the post-Nirvana indie-rock feeding frenzy among the major labels—for strict independence and low ticket and record prices. *The Washington Post* once wrote that Fugazi's "rigid adherence to these precepts gives the band that most valuable of intangibles: integrity."

Still, that integrity has a very tangible reward: money. Fugazi alone has sold over 1 million records. While MacKaye wouldn't discuss total income for his label or band, I run a small indie rock label myself and have some sense of the costs involved. Even given overhead that's much higher than mine (Dischord has a half dozen employees who receive a full panoply of health and other benefits), I can't figure that Fugazi is netting any less than $2.50 per CD, and probably more. (The issue is complicated because Dischord's bands are paid a pure profit split, and MacKaye is both part owner of the label and a band member.) From there, the math isn't hard. Having the integrity to collect all of the money off your work leaves you with something more than just integrity to take to the bank.

That doesn't mean that making the money was your main goal,

which is the distinction important to MacKaye—and he is definitely sincere. "Rock 'n' roll is an insidious collision between art and business," he tells me. "I'm in this parallel but valid industry and I'm self-sufficient. I just feel much more comfortable doing it this way. It makes more sense, and I understand the air here."

MacKaye proudly describes how he grew up in D.C., a town the record industry ignored, and built a thriving company off his own band's efforts and savings. As a young man in his first band, the Teen Idles, he was "disgusted by the way the rock 'n' roll industry worked. It was all packaged and had no organic aspect. Then I came across punk rock, and I felt comfortable here. Profit isn't the final motive in punk rock. People's ambitions were much more creative. It's not to make money, it's to play with ideas. Making money is an addiction that is very tedious." Of course, making money can make "playing with ideas" easier, and spread those ideas farther, as Hughes, the Gainesville record store owner, tried to explain to the amateur record-label owners.

"Profit isn't the final motive in punk rock."

Despite his concerns over the addiction of money making, MacKaye is—as he should be—comfortable with his own money. "I'm confident that I'm responsible and am doing things that are useful and reinvesting in things I can believe in," MacKaye says. Fugazi's success allows him to support other local D.C. bands on Dischord that only sell 3,000 records.

Ms. magazine cover girl Ani DiFranco is the current sensation of the radically indie philosophy in music. She told *The Washington Post* that the music business is "dehumanizing and exploitative"—and "not much different from any other big business," so she sells her records through her own Buffalo-based label, Righteous Babe Records. *Forbes,* praising her business savvy, reports that she pulls in an average net of $4.25 per CD sold, with 260,000 sold in 1996. The Artist Formerly Known as Prince, who mused publicly about going totally indie after his acrimonious split with Warner Brothers, but instead now runs his own NPG Records through a manufacturing and distribution deal with EMI/Capitol, said it best to *Forbes*: "I *love* Ani DiFranco. She's making $4 a record and the superstars are making $2, so who's got the better deal?"

And the superstars are doing a lot better than smaller-sales artists like DiFranco could realistically hope to on major labels. Typical new artist royalties amount to around $1.30 per unit, says New Jersey musicians' manager Gary Waldman, who was vice president of MegaForce Records in the '80s. And those royalties only kick in after, on average, 300,000 units sold, because big labels charge all recording fees, advances, production costs, and most promotional and touring costs against artist royalties.

On a major label, an artist can easily sell as many records as DiFranco and still not see a penny past the initial advance. *The Buffalo News* writes that DiFranco is about "talent, art and integrity winning out over the usual record business pitfalls of hype, money and conformity." DiFranco is a nonconformist. But, says Waldman, "Ani DiFranco is making a much better living than she would through a major label." The truly cash-minded, greedy musician would do well to nonconform along with Ani. And with her leading the way, it is increasingly possible that some superstar on the Prince level will take the financial risks of going indie to reap the possibly greater rewards. (The risks include both the upfront money the artists would have to pay for recording and manufacturing, and the less-than-perfect distribution and promotion system for indies—though the more superstars go that route, the better the distribution would become.)

I ask Dischord's MacKaye whether, given the realities of major label financing, he thinks Fugazi could conceivably do better financially with a major—whether his business decisions not only fit with his independent sensibilities but make good financial sense as well. "That's too hypothetical a question." he responds sharply. "I don't give a [expletive]. I don't spend my time trying to compare relative incomes of various possibilities." He then goes on to explain how Dischord began from his pure motive to do what he wanted to do. Granted. But as much as I respect MacKaye for sticking to his principles, it seems strange that he is so reluctant even to discuss the financial benefits that follow his principles. Those benefits are an integral part of small-business capitalism, even if MacKaye's punk rock background doesn't encourage defending that dirty word.

The tension between entrepreneurial reality and anti-capitalist ideology is becoming increasingly apparent in indie art. Since the early '80s, the 'zine *Maximum Rock 'n' Roll* has been the Bible for young punks—the main ideological enforcer of the anti-money, anti-corporate line in amateur punk rock and the place where younger fans learn what it means to be properly punk. The Berkeley-based 'zine used to run a column by Lawrence Livermore, former operator of the indie punk label Lookout! Records. When Lookout! artists Green Day hit it big, and the company began making millions (though Green Day left them for Warner Brothers), the *MRR* crowd turned on Lookout! with such ferocity that a weary Livermore sold his interest in the label and left punk rock behind, announcing his defection in a column in *Punk Planet*, a rival 'zine founded in 1994. By contrast, *Punk Planet* sees Lookout!'s success as a triumph.

"They made money by putting out good records. I don't think they should be faulted, they should be heralded," *Punk Planet*'s editor, Daniel Sinker, insists. "Now their employees have health insurance and the bands are getting paid well. The difference between them and the majors is that the majors don't exist to put out good music—they are just arms of major corporations to make money for it. They wouldn't care if it's records or microwave ovens."

Sinker believes in companies that care about music over

money. (He refuses ads from major labels.) But he recognizes that the business of selling music, however small-scale and independent, is, well, a business. *Punk Planet* ran a long March/April cover story analyzing what Sinker calls the "lie of punk"—the notion that punk rock exists in a Platonic realm of purity, in opposition to the dirt and greed of capitalism. "You have to bludgeon people over the head with the idea that making and selling records is capitalist, and that's what punks do," Sinker says. *Punk Planet*, with its more realistic attitude toward commerce, has risen in sales from 800 copies of its first issue to 7,000 now. (*MRR* sells 13,000.)

Often in indie pop culture, people try to disguise business realities. But acknowledging it can encourage institutions that protect artistic control without eschewing commerce and, in turn, expand the opportunities to create art. Peter Bagge draws the popular alternative comic *Hate* for the small publisher Fantagraphics. While he doesn't self-publish—he doesn't want to cope with all the necessary business details—artists who work for Fantagraphics do retain ownership of their characters and art. (This is true of many newer, smaller comic book publishers.) Fantagraphics pays its artists purely royalties based on sales and retains a small percentage interest in merchandising, though the artist has approval over merchandising deals.

"Often in indie pop culture, people try to disguise business realities."

For a long time Fantagraphics didn't run outside advertisements in its comics, assuming that its sensitive artists would object to this invasion of commerce into their realm. That wasn't always true. "When I found out I could get more pages in my comic and keep the price steady by running ads, I said, absolutely!" says Bagge. "If I knew I stood to gain, I would have done it from issue one." Now Bagge's comic book features more pages, but with the same cover price. He uses those extra ad-driven pages to run backup features by other artists, thus exposing them to his larger audience. Many of his fellow Fantagraphics artists have followed suit on the ad question, although some are still holding out.

Bagge has been on the receiving end of shouts of "sellout!" from purist fans for changing his comic to color from black-and-white, for running ads, for adding UPC codes to the cover. He expects more such carping if he seals the deal he's working on to sell a cartoon based on his characters to a cable network. "If I tell my next door neighbor, who doesn't care about the comic book world, he'll say, 'Great!' He'll be disappointed if it *doesn't* happen," Bagge says. "But among the comic book people, I'll hear all sorts of nasty comments, and almost to a man people criticizing me will be doing it from resentment."

More than just resentment is at stake, though. Advocates of independence often believe in the propriety of what they do on an ideological level that goes beyond just business sense. For example, a leading small comic publisher, Caliber, and a leading indie record label, Simple Machines, both issue pamphlets explaining step-by-step how individuals can manufacture comics or records themselves. This is not usual corporate practice, to say the least—actively instructing your customers on how to compete with you or do without you.

Audiences for smaller-circulation music and comics often feel special because of the pop culture they choose, set apart from the thoughtless throng. This attitude can be self-indulgent, a way to prop oneself up at the expense of the herdlike masses. As a reader of indie comics and a producer *and* consumer of indie rock music, however, I know there are often-important aesthetic distinctions between small-company and self-produced pop culture and the larger mass pop culture. Without getting into extended aesthetic arguments, music outside the limited range of commercial sounds available on contemporary rock radio is just more interesting and exciting. When SST Records, a 1980s indie rock powerhouse and early home for such bands as Sonic Youth, Dinosaur Jr., Soundgarden, and the Meat Puppets, sold bumper stickers reading "Corporate Rock Sucks!" they meant it for both business and aesthetic reasons.

That punk rock attitude has spread throughout most underground youth culture arts; the audiences for underground music and comics largely overlap. As comic book artist Evan Dorkin once told *The Comics Journal,* "People who like stuff that's hard to find tend to like stuff that's hard to find in every medium. They just develop this attitude that, 'I'm not going to find my stuff at Tower Records, at B. Dalton's bookstore.'"

Meanwhile, the community aspect of the independent arts adds a level of non-cash-oriented play to these small markets—an aspect that is often hidden in big corporate capitalism. The richer our world becomes through the workings of capitalism, the more considerations of play can work alongside the bloodless financial calculations that prompt cries of "sellout!" from indie purists.

After years of refining their tastes—and becoming jaded about the often crude pleasures of more mainstream rock and comics—certain cognoscenti are indeed going to find more pleasure in small-circulation products for aesthetic reasons that go beyond mere snobbery. But anti-mass-market snobbery is hard to get rid of. In Washington, D.C., various indie labels get together for an annual "Indie Rock Flea Market" in which bands play, food is served, and labels and bands set up tables and sell records. In 1994, the local "commercial alternative" station—anathema to the true-blue indie rock fan—set up a booth. Two indie fans were disgusted, *The Washington Post* reported: "The mass marketing of their beloved subculture has devalued its music."

Such snobbery ignores some of the real benefits of money for small pop cultures. Ian MacKaye's Fugazi money supports many other bands. The money made by one of the creators of *Teenage Mutant Ninja Turtles,* of all mass-market excrescences (though it too began as a self-published parody of mutant comic books, not the kids' sensation it became), supports the Xeric Foundation, which gives grants to destitute young comic book artists to allow them to self-publish. The relationship between capitalism and lively underground culture can be complex.

The comments of one of the organizers of the Indie Rock Flea Market are revealing: "I just wanted to create a venue where the demographics were all the same, where everyone liked the same stuff."

"Everyone liking the same stuff" is the language of the fan seeking an isolated, small, simpatico community, one of the driving values behind small, alternative artistic subcultures. "Demographics" is the language of people trying to sell you something. They can mean the same thing. One does not rule out the other—and doesn't everyone, creator and audience, benefit from being able to buy the things we want?

As Gary Groth, owner of Bagge's publisher, Fantagraphics, and editor of *The Comics Journal*, puts it: "A lot of anti-corporate talk can basically be self-serving greed. It's just another new market: the anti-corporate market."

Take Me Out to the Boardroom[6]

Peter O'Malley sounds like a man who's tired of the fight. His family has owned the Los Angeles Dodgers for 47 years—a longer tenure than any other ownership group in Major League Baseball—but earlier in the year he stunned the sports industry by announcing that the team, one of baseball's crown jewels, was for sale. It is a sunny afternoon in May, and in a few days O'Malley will make a deal with Rupert Murdoch's News Corp., selling the team for an extraordinary $350 million, the most ever paid for a sports franchise. In March 1998, Rupert Murdoch became the owner of the Los Angeles Dodgers.

But on this particular day O'Malley is troubled. He's a baseball man, after all. Running the team has been his fulltime job—practically his only job—and the Dodgers franchise has also been the O'Malley clan's primary investment. Yet as a family business, baseball has become almost absurdly expensive and contentious. Labor wars. Rising salaries. Marketing ineptitude. Disappearing fans. A commissioner? Please. For O'Malley it is time to cash out and leave the headaches to someone more battle-ready. Someone who can afford to ride out the squalls of the tempestuous sports scene. Someone who might bring some fiscal discipline to the sport. Someone who can afford to pay him what he wants. O'Malley knows that that someone will almost certainly be a corporation.

"Corporate ownership is the way of the future, and I think that's good," O'Malley says, looking out at the field from his wood-paneled office inside Dodger Stadium. "I think it was [the late Chicago Cubs owner] Phil Wrigley who said that baseball is too much of a sport to be a business and too much of a business to be a sport, and golly, he was right on target. The last four years have been very tough for fans, players, owners, executives, everyone. In many cases, corporations have a greater sense of responsibility and more financial stability—as well as fewer personal agendas—than some of the individuals who have bought franchises, and that appeals to me a lot. Corporate ownership is good for sports."

Good or bad, it is revolutionizing the economics of professional sports. Once the sale of the Dodgers is approved by baseball owners—and they will approve it, despite Murdoch's running feud with Ted Turner—News Corp. will become one of 52 public companies owning at least a slice of the 113 Major League Baseball, National Basketball Association, or National Hockey League franchises (the NFL doesn't allow corporations to own teams, at least for now). Once a playground for the rich, pro

---

6 Article by Roy S. Johnson, from *Fortune* 139/2:42-47. Reprinted from the July 21, 1997, issue of Fortune by special permission.

sports is swiftly becoming a company picnic. "Almost total corporate ownership is an inevitability," says Leigh Steinberg, the influential agent. "It's a trend that can be delayed but not reversed. Leagues can resist it. They can create rules trying to discourage it, but ultimately the nature of the sports-entertainment matrix will demand it."

Murdoch, in fact, is staking claims on the sports landscape as if he were in the Oklahoma Land Rush. While still crunching the numbers on the Dodgers deal, he actually ended up owning pieces of the New York Knicks and the New York Rangers as part of an $850 million investment in Rainbow Media, the sports programming arm of Cablevision Systems. (Murdoch is expected to sell his stakes in the New York teams to clear the way to purchase two teams closer to corporate headquarters: the Los Angeles Kings and a portion of the Los Angeles Lakers. That way he'll have the part of Southern California that doesn't already belong to Disney, owner of the Anaheim Mighty Ducks and 25% of the Angels.)

"Sports franchises are quickly becoming the core asset in the sports communications business..."

Beyond the sheer numbers, the News Corp. deals are emblematic of a deeper change: Sports franchises are quickly becoming *the* core asset in the sports communications business, and the longball hitters are getting into the game. Murdoch's arrival creates a true Murderers' Row of powerful media and entertainment companies in the owner's boxes. Leading off with Tribune Co., which purchased the Cubs back in 1981, the lineup now includes Disney, Time Warner (Atlanta Braves and Hawks, and the NHL expansion Atlanta Thrashers, who begin play in 1999), Comcast (Philadelphia 76ers and Flyers), and Cablevision.

What attracts these companies is a powerful mix of potential strategic alliances: a growing need for live-event programming in a zillion-channel broadcast, cable, and satellite universe; the emergence of sports franchises as solid "brands" that can be exploited in numerous ways; and the opportunity to blend sports with the companies' entertainment properties in stadium and arena complexes where the game is only one of many attractions. "Our main goal is to get people to spend their disposable income with properties associated with the company, whether they're our theme parks, videos, movies, or our sports teams," says Tony Tavares, president of Disney's Anaheim Sports. "If you've got a dollar, we want it." To put it another way: An entertainment brand is really a set of managed allegiances, and there's no quicker way to forge an allegiance than by purchasing fandom.

"What else can you go out and buy today that's a living, breathing example of tradition and loyalty?" says Mark B. Mahoney, who heads the investment banking division at First Union, which has represented many companies seeking to tap into the sports industry. "A film library? A music collection? That's about it. Besides, how much would it cost for any company to go out and build a brand on its own? It's easier—and probably cheaper—to simply buy something everybody already likes."

For all these reasons, a sports franchise has an entirely different kind of value for a corporate owner than it does for a family or an old-fashioned syndicate. If annual profitability is what you're after, you're better off with a Burger King franchise than with a sports team. Soaring salaries will likely force almost half the National Basketball Association teams into the red for this season, despite an expected increase in league revenues to $1.5 billion this season from $1.3 billion in 1995–96. In baseball, teams lost in aggregate between $200 million and $300 million last season. "Operating the team is essentially the same business it was in the 1920s; you sell tickets and hot dogs," says Stan Kasten, president of the Hawks and Braves. "And there's only so many you can sell. It's not like Microsoft, which can grow a million-dollar business into a $50 billion business."

The Dodgers, for instance, had $13.5 million in operating income last year on revenue of $75 million. Does that justify a price that's about 30 times earnings? Sure, if you're a conglomerate with plans to conquer the world, not just win the World Series. Compared with News Corp.'s $10 billion in annual revenues, the purchase price of the Dodgers looks like a rounding error. "So what if a huge company overpays by $25 million or so," says Mahoney. "It's nothing. Immaterial. Fundamentally, cash flows are generally low in comparison to values, but companies are not buying for value, they're buying the underlying software. The payout's in the pipeline."

No kidding. Baseball as a fully leveraged asset bears hardly any resemblance to what you may recall as a quiet day at the ballpark with Dad. The $242.5 million Turner Field in Atlanta, the Braves' new world, is a testament to what lies ahead: interactive cyberball. You can pitch and hit in simulated games, use electronic kiosks to peruse scouting reports on 300 current and former Braves or watch any other Major League game in progress on one of the televisions in the Clubhouse Store. Big screens show live locker-room interviews, and there is enough fiberoptic cable buried underneath the place to allow games to be broadcast live anywhere on the planet. Kids can frolic with Bugs Bunny, Foghorn Leghorn, and other Warner Bros. cartoon characters in the children's areas. And oh, yeah, the Braves play there too.

As a business, baseball is learning what basketball has known for more than a decade. "I talk about the NBA as having 29 'theme parks,' cable distribution, a consumer products business, publishing interests, trading cards, and sponsorship relationships," says league commissioner David Stern, in his Manhattan office overlooking Fifth Avenue. "Those are areas that are attractive to the people at any major company. With that combination of opportunities, plus the increasing value of the franchises themselves, it was inevitable that you would soon move toward an ownership mix of the Fortune 500 and people among, if you'll pardon the expression, the *Forbes* 400."

Since 1990 the cost of entry to the NBA has quadrupled. That year the Orlando Magic and Minnesota Timberwolves paid $32.5 million each as expansion teams. Two years ago the Toronto Raptors and Vancouver Grizzlies anted up a whopping $125 million each to join the party. In baseball, Baltimore businessman Peter Angelos and a group of investors (among them novelist Tom Clancy and former tennis star Pam Shriver) purchased the Baltimore Orioles four years ago for the then handsome sum of $193 million. In light of the Dodgers' deal, the Orioles could likely command much more if they were for sale.

"Individuals are simply being priced out of the marketplace, unless they're infatuated with the thought of owning a team," says Jerry Colangelo, president and CEO of the Phoenix Suns and part owner of just about every sports property in the city, including the baseball expansion Diamondbacks and the Coyotes hockey franchise. "But that will become a more and more expensive toy."

"Teams were wearing the names of local businesses on their uniforms as long ago as the turn of the century."

Corporate owners aren't new to pro sports, of course. Teams were wearing the names of local businesses on their uniforms as long ago as the turn of the century. Big business stepped up to the plate in 1953, when Anheuser-Busch bought the St. Louis Cardinals.

Big media first entered the game in 1964, when CBS purchased 80% of the New York Yankees for $11.2 million (later it bought the rest for $2 million). But a ball team was just a ball team back then; the breathtaking TV deals were still more than 20 years away. Licensing and apparel sales were in their infancy. Autographs were free. Nine years later, with the Yankees faltering, CBS sold the team to a partnership of wealthy individuals led by a bombastic shipbuilder named Steinbrenner. The price tag: $10 million. Nice investment, guys.

A few years later, Turner, then a fledgling entrepreneur, had this zany idea of building a national television network out of a tiny UHF station by beaming its signal to cable systems around the country via the emerging satellite technology. Lacking much juicy programming, Turner had another radical thought: Buy the Braves and the Hawks, slap them on the bird and let 'em fly. So began the "superstation," which ultimately begot a slew of broadcast properties known as Turner Broadcasting System, acquired last year by Time Warner (corporate parent of Fortune's publisher). Turner is now Time Warner's vice chairman.

That strategy will never be repeated: Each league now controls the national and international television rights to its teams, so an owner today can't use the franchise as national programming the way Turner did. Today the opportunities lie in local and regional programming.

Enter Murdoch, the guy who likes to change the rules of every game he plays. The guy who dropped a bomb into the middle of the NFL's television negotiations three years ago by offering a staggering $1.58 billion to broadcast National Football Conference games. Today his Fox network also shares the national broadcast rights for Major League Baseball (it airs a third of all baseball games televised). Now he's at it again. With the Cablevision move, Murdoch makes the sports cable game a real slugfest.

The king of sports cable at the moment is Disney's ESPN, which reaches 71 million homes and carries only national programming. Murdoch is betting that on most nights, fans would rather watch their home team than a nationally televised game between two other teams. In a joint venture with TCI, he is stitching together a network of 20 regional cable outlets, called Fox Sports Net, that televise local teams.

Once the deal's done, FSN will own the regional rights to 49 pro teams and reach 55 million households nationwide. Since telecasts of the home team usually earn higher ratings locally than games televised nationally, Murdoch will be able to offer national advertisers a unique alternative to ESPN: a customized package of regional advertising that could, in aggregate, reach an audience bigger than what ESPN's national telecasts draw. Also, Fox Sports Net will be able to sell the kind of local and regional advertising ESPN can't. "It'll take some time for Fox to find its programming stride, but obviously ESPN will be looking over its shoulder," says Mike Garofolo, vice president of local sports for Zenith Media, a division of Saatchi & Saatchi Advertising.

How does owning the Dodgers, and possibly the Lakers and Kings, fit into this strategy? Unlike national and international rights, a team's local and regional rights can be exploited freely by the owner. And live sports is some of the most valuable programming in the land. "Our business has become more and more event-driven, and sporting events are second to none," says News Corp. co-chief operating officer Chase Carey. "Sports will have a more and more important role in our business. That's part of what justifies our belief in this move."

Not all corporate team owners have quite so elaborate a game plan, but all are looking for leverage of one kind or another. The beer synergy endures: Coors owns part of the Colorado Rockies, Interbrew SA of Belgium has a stake in the Toronto Blue Jays, and Molson owns the Montreal Canadians. (Anheuser-Busch sold the Cardinals last year, but it still owns the NHL's St. Louis Blues.)

Other potential owners are forming corporate versions of the old-fashioned syndicates of rich individuals, putting together groups of local companies to either buy an existing team or attract an expansion team to give a boost to the regional economy. That was the pitch Jerry Colangelo made when he began approaching Phoenix-area companies four years ago about forging a partnership that would ultimately bid for a Major League Baseball expansion franchise. Fourteen businesses eventually helped forge a group that pledged $300 million, which the lords of baseball couldn't resist. What was the attraction for the locals, who could certainly have found other, more profitable places to stash their cash than in the Diamondbacks? "I think it was a situation where the private sector invested simply to add to the quality of life in the area," Colangelo says. "All of them, for instance, are competing for talent, just as the teams are. And just as we think this is a city where athletes will like to play, our investors believe that the presence of sports will make Phoenix an attraction for their own potential employees as well."

Beer and boosterism will always have their place in sports, but it is the big media companies that have shown other owners how their teams can play in a larger arena. In Toronto, Isaiah Thomas has a vision for the Raptors that extends far beyond winning an NBA championship: He wants the team's dinosaur mascot to become "the Mickey Mouse of the sports world." (Remember when that phrase would have meant the very opposite of an ambitious dream?) The former all-star guard has owned 9% of the two-year-old team since its inception, and he currently heads a group of investors, Chase Manhattan among them, that's trying to purchase the controlling interest. "I don't see the Raptors as just a basketball team," Thomas says. "I see them as one day being the centerpiece of an entertainment entity. Our intention is to make this a $1 billion company. Even now our corporate culture is to create an environment in every division similar to what Disney has done."

"'...our corporate culture is to create an environment in every division similar to what Disney has done.'"

The Raptors may be the only "ride" in Thomas' proto-Disney so far, but already he's thinking in terms of the sports-entertainment matrix. "I want to be able to preserve the sheer enjoyment a fan gets when he walks through the door, sits down, and buys a hot dog from a vender," he says. "They should experience that true joy, not what I feel when I close a business deal. In Disneyland you're in Mickey's World, not Michael Eisner's."

Take a good look around. Take a deep breath. Take your kids. Dodger Stadium won't feel like this much longer. The view from O'Malley's office is a window to an era when natural grass, one-run games, and a Dodger Dog were enough. There are no luxury boxes. No corporate logos plastered everywhere—just an inconspicuous Coca-Cola sign atop a pole in center field.

It is a special place, and the Dodgers are a special team: winners of six World Series, breakers of baseball's color barrier, the team of Koufax and Drysdale. "We have an extraordinary tradition, and we respect it, nurture it," O'Malley says. "Our reputation is unique and we want to enhance it. We're proud of it, and it's very important to all of us."

News Corp.'s Carey and Peter Chernin, the company's other co-COO, will be charged with preserving what's special about the

Dodgers. They're on the hot seat, and they know it. Screw this Dodger thing up, and FOX is fur. Yes, they'll start building sky boxes as soon as the deal is ratified, and yes, they'll welcome corporate sponsorship and advertising. But no, Bart Simpson will not throw out the first pitch of the new regime. "We'll be far less intrusive than others," says Chernin, a former New Yorker who grew up a fan of the Brooklyn Dodgers. "We know the Dodgers represent something special to the people in the city, evoking an era of nostalgia that resonates from Jackie Robinson to Hideo Nomo." Adds Carey, a longtime Yankee fan: "This is a wonderful opportunity to build upon something that already resonates with its fans. With some of our other businesses, that's the hardest part."

There will be a few speed bumps as the sports industry barrels toward corporate ownership. Conflict of interest, for instance. During negotiations for national broadcast and cable rights, three media company/owners will be represented on both sides of the table. FOX and Fox Sports Net, ESPN, and Time Warner's WTBS and TNT all figure to vie for some portion of the broadcast or cable rights whenever any of the league's current contracts expire. The rights are now negotiated by committees made up of a handful of owners, but as more and more corporations buy franchises, it may become increasingly difficult to screen out the potential conflicts.

Another bump: Each of the leagues has rules preventing owners from circumventing salary-cap regulations by offering "side deals" like stock, options, or movie deals to players. But who's to say some of the major media companies, with their television and movie units, won't be more attractive to an agent looking to sign his client with a team that offers a few (wink, wink) "post-career opportunities?" Leigh Steinberg calls the notion "tempting." NBA team executives, for instance, must sign affidavits stating they won't cut such deals. But if Michael Jordan ambles into Jerry Reinsdorf's office and asks for a piece of the Chicago Bulls in exchange for playing another season, what's the guy supposed to say? *You haven't earned it, Michael. Sorry.*

Major bump: Do the math. As successful financially as Major League Baseball, the NHL, and the NBA may claim to be, their annual revenues are no match for those of many of the large corporations whose teams they must govern. Could the big dogs someday plot to take over the pound? Fear of such a putsch was at the heart of the NFL's decision to ban corporate ownership decades ago. "We've always had the view that the ultimate value of our franchises is in being part of the overall operation," says Stern. "If you deteriorate into anarchy and are unwilling to check your corporate identity at the door, you're going to wind up with a very damaged asset that won't be able to compete globally."

Traditionalists will warn that the big, bad corporate Cuisinart will ultimately grind sports fans' cherished games into pulp.

Decisions will be made with the stock price in mind, not the final score. The number crunchers will force the team's general manager—the guy who knows sports—to pass on the high-priced free agent because, well, the numbers didn't work. Fans will be assaulted with nine innings of "It's a Small World," four quarters of *Batman and Robin* previews, or three periods of insipid scenes from *Party of Five*.

Relax. It's not likely. Let's face it, many of the sports industry's current ills—public bickering between players and management, nomadic franchises and fiscal irresponsibility, to name a few—can be blamed largely on the few egotistical individual owners who allow personal agendas to override the good of their sport. In fact, corporate owners would probably never commit the sin of moving a franchise—the bane of the fan's existence. Why? Does Michael Eisner realty need a bunch of rabid fans picketing at Disneyland?

"Some rich guy who believes he has only a five- to seven-year window in which to win will spend almost any kind of money to do so," says Peter Ueberroth, the former baseball commissioner. "Corporations will tend to be more responsible. Operating records will be more public and thus available to communities and fans. Ultimately they are more responsible to shareholders than to fans, which should bring some reasonableness to the cost of salaries." It's a nice thought, but probably not a very realistic one. Hasn't at least one of the media companies that also owns a sports franchise paid Demi Moore $20 million to star in a movie?

There is reason to believe that in the end, not much will change when it comes to what matters most—winning. Most successful corporations and the people who run them are as competitive as they come. If it comes down to signing the free-agent 20-game winner for $50 million or meeting the Wall Street analysts' estimates, well, which way are the new corporate owners likely to swing? "Do we need to make money?" asks Terry McGuirk, president and CEO of Turner Broadcasting System, which oversees the Braves and Hawks. "Yes, we try to. Do we always? No. But we take a lot of value in winning, and sometimes we're willing to sacrifice profits in order to achieve that."

III. The Corporate Gift

Editor's Introduction

The third section of this compilation discusses the power inherent to the corporate gift or donation. As corporations control vast sums of money that can be spent or donated essentially at their discretion, they enjoy a considerable degree of power within a variety of arenas, including government, education, the arts, and charities. It follows that the corporate donation is perhaps one of the most tangible signs of both positive and negative corporate power. On the negative side, critics question the corporation's motive behind the donation, as well as the control the corporation has over the recipient of that donation. On the positive side, the corporate donation can enable advances in medicine, art, and education that may not have been otherwise possible. Here, articles discuss the extent of those contributions, as well as the mixed reactions they evoke.

Currently, debate rages over the issue of political campaign financing. The authors of the first article in this section point out that since 1904 it has been illegal for the corporation to fund a candidate's campaign for office. Lawmakers wanted to prevent candidates from placing the needs of the corporation before the needs of the constituency they serve once that candidate was elected. Rather than donate directly to the candidate's campaign, corporations are forced to donate money to the candidate's party. While the candidate's party is similarly "prevented from using it to campaign directly for their presidential and congressional candidate," the authors argue that there are a variety of loopholes through which the candidate's party can use the corporate donation to in fact influence the outcome of elections.The corporate donation, as it is not a direct donation to the candidate, is thus termed "soft money." Many fear that it represents an extension of corporate power that gets politicians to place the needs of the corporation over the needs of the public. In this article, the authors discuss the debate surrounding "soft money," its effect on party budgets and candidate campaigns, and efforts to reform campaign donation legislation.

John H. Cushman Jr., writing for *The New York Times,* discusses the effects of corporate giving to the National Governors' Association. According to Cushman, donations made by the corporation to the National Governors' Association ("about $786,000 in 1996") allow corporate lobbyists to gain access to the committee meetings and research organizations in which legislation is discussed and honed. Many, however, sharply disagree that such access allows corporate lobbyists any real influence on the laws that are made.

The following article, also from *The New York Times,* describes the concept of strategic corporate giving. According to the author, corporations no longer donate money or goods indiscriminately. Instead, they tend to give to causes that "mesh with the company's markets or employees." For example Avon products now only donates "to programs that relate specifically to women," as the majority of their customers are women. This is not to say that corporations are giving less. The author notes that corporate donations increased from $7.9 billion in 1995 to $8.5 billion in 1996. As this money is strategically donated, however, the relationship between marketing, public relations, and corporate giving is more evident.

On a more positive tone, Jan Jarboe Russell gives an account of the vast sums of money corporations have donated to breast cancer research. Since 1989, Revlon alone "has given more than $12 million for research." Cash giving, however, is not the only form of corporate donation. The Y-Me organization, essentially a hotline that provides free counseling for women with breast cancer, received telephone and computer upgrades from the Boston Market fast-food chain. As a result, Y-Me is able to counsel over 60 percent more women than before. It's clear that corporate donations, if effectively applied, empower the corporation to benefit those causes and efforts that have significant impact on the lives of many in need.

The last article in this section, "Miracle on 42nd St." by Bruce Handy, discusses Disney's rehabilitation of New York City's Times Square area. While Disney's cleanup of Times Square is not a corporate donation, it has succeeded in transforming a former prostitution, drug-peddling, and porn theater haven into a tourist attraction. In need of a theater to house *Beauty and the Beast*, Disney C.E.O. Michael Eisner negotiated with New York City for the old, and then dilapidated, New Amersterdam theater, which is situated next to Times Square. The deal was made, the theater was transformed, and the rest of Times Square followed suit. Musicals and tourism now flourish in an area once noted for its crime and vice. In many ways, the cleanup of Times Square is Disney's gift to the people of New York City as well as a testament to the benefits of corporate financial power that is correctly applied.

The Country Club[1]

How an elite group of corporations, unions and super-rich individuals is financing the political parties, shaping the political agenda and reaping great rewards with huge soft money contributions.

Swanee Hunt is a member. So are Daniel Abraham, the Slim Fast man, and Darrell Issa, whose scary voice warns unwitting passersby that they've committed a "perimeter violation" of cars outfitted with the Viper alarm system. Chiquita banana man Carl Lindner is a charter member, as is soybean magnate Dwayne Andreas. There's even a former U.S. citizen on the roster, an 84-year-old tuna king who went to England to avoid the IRS, along with a couple of Cuban-exile brothers who own and run a huge chunk of southern Florida but have never become U.S. citizens. Why bother voting when you can simply buy your way into the political system?

In a roundabout way, Mickey Mouse is also a member, as is Joe Camel. Steven "E.T." Spielberg and Barbra "Like Butter" Streisand add a touch of glitter and glamour to the ranks, but most of the members are all business. Big business, small business, bigger-than-many-countries businesses. Throw in some labor bosses, all the tobacco titans, a couple of former soap salesmen, lots of money mavens, plenty of oil tycoons, land and liquor types, some high-powered media moguls, the telephone people, the drug lords, a few gamblers, health providers and a layer of lawyers, and the member profile of the national country club begins to come into focus.

The one thing all members of the country club have in common is a history of signing very large checks made payable to the Republican and Democratic parties. They also share a remarkably uncommon level of access to and influence with the country's top elected officials, and have been known to frequent White House dinners and win special favors from practically every outpost of the federal government. Several of them, including oil heiress Hunt, now go by the title "ambassador" or "Cabinet secretary."

The term "country club" is not a new one in political discourse. Republicans have long been referred to as the country club set, and more recent references to country club Republicans have sought to distinguish the blue-blooded establishment types from Pat Buchanan's blue-collared rabble-rousers. But thanks to the influence of increasingly huge and widely used unregulated "soft money" contributions to the political parties, a new country club

---

[1] Article by Vicki Kemper, editor, and Deborah Lutterbeck, staff writer, from *Common Cause* 22/1:16-35 Spr/Sum '96. Copyright © 1996 Common Cause. Reprinted with permission.

has taken root: a club of wealthy, high-powered donors who help set the political agenda, impact the outcomes and, in many ways, run the country.

From January 1991, when federal election law first required the disclosure of their contributions, through 1995, country club members poured more than $229 million into the Republican and Democratic parties; more than half of that five-year total was contributed in the past two years alone. And the cumulative total of soft money contributions from 1988 is at least $292 million. But donors have reaped billions of dollars' worth of government subsidies, business deals, tax provisions and regulatory reforms.

The members of this ever-growing group of big political donors come from virtually every segment of the nation's economy: Their products fill our pantries, medicine cabinets and gas tanks; they hold and invest our money. They control the health care system, rule Wall Street, dominate the entertainment industry, run the television and cable networks and virtually all the long-distance companies, operate the gambling casinos, clog the courts, do our accounting, build our cars, fly our airlines, provide us with everything from greeting cards to liquor, own the stores where we shop, the restaurants where we dine and the professional sports teams we cheer on. They often pollute the air we breathe and the water we drink. They even hire us and lay us off.

"From January 1991...through 1995 country club members poured more than $229 million into the Republican and Democratic parties..."

And they are just as ubiquitous in the political system. Whether the issue is tobacco regulation, trade, the minimum wage, energy policy, education, agriculture subsidies, telecommunications law, taxes, environmental controls, health care reform, antitrust rules, drug approval, legal reform or workplace safety, club members make their voices heard. Contributors say they give hundreds of thousands—sometimes millions—of dollars as a form of political insurance, to make sure they're in the room and at the table when agendas are set, issues are discussed, bills are written, votes are cast, appointments are made and compromises are hammered out.

Many club members are also buying party insurance, making large contributions to both political parties to guarantee access, influence and agenda-setting power no matter who's in the White House or which party controls Congress. There are 254 of these "double donors"; five of them merit membership in the exclusive $2 million club. Philip Morris Co. Inc., Archer Daniels Midland Co. (ADM), RJR Nabisco Inc., American Financial Corp. and Atlantic Richfield Co. (ARCO), along with their executives and subsidiaries, have each contributed a total of more than $2 million in soft money since January 1991.

Another five contributors—Joseph E. Seagram & Sons Inc., the National Education Association, U.S. Tobacco Co., Chevron Corp. and Merrill Lynch & Co. Inc.—make the millionaires' circle, having contributed more than $1 million in soft money from January 1991 through 1995.

Amway Corp. is in a league of its own, having contributed $2.5

million to the Republicans on a single day shortly before the 1994 midterm elections. The company gave the GOP another $60,000 in 1995, and contributions from Amway executives bring the company's total contributions to more than $2.8 million, making it the country's No. 1 soft money contributor.

Other leading categories of contributors of $20,000 or more in soft money from January 1991 include financial interests, with $29.5 million in contributions; manufacturers, $20 million; oil, gas and energy interests, $15 million; miscellaneous businesses, $11.3 million; labor unions, $11.1 million; food and agriculture, $10.6 million; and real estate interests, $9.8 million. Tobacco companies, telecommunications firms, lawyers, media conglomerates and financial interests have been among the largest contributors in the past year.

While more traditional clubs have various membership requirements and restrictions, anyone can join the country's soft money club—as long as they have the cash. Among its members are the entire U.S. tobacco industry; four of the country's "Big Six" accounting firms; most of Wall Street; the world's biggest oil, natural gas and wine companies; owners of all four major television networks; the world's two largest garbage haulers; the country's largest soft-drink makers and greeting card sellers; the nation's biggest owner of cable TV systems; the country's largest agribusinesses and drug companies; and many of the country's most popular retail outlets.

But many country club members have also run into trouble with the law. They've been investigated, sued for and convicted of everything from price-fixing and false advertising to marketing faulty products, violating labor and immigration laws, engaging in anticompetitive behavior, polluting and nonpayment of taxes. The country club's roster also includes many of the nation's unemployers; AT&T, Sears Roebuck & Co., Digital Equipment, GTE, Nynex, Delta Airlines and Chemical Banking/Chase Manhattan are just some of the corporations who've made huge political contributions while laying off tens of thousands of employees. And with every new round of corporate mergers and buyouts, the club's roster has to be updated.

Club members are many things, but they are not us—not if we are the 99.97 percent of Americans who don't make political contributions of more than $200. Yet more and more it is big-moneyed special interests who are calling the political shots, analysts say, and their interests are not always ours.

While the soft money club was created by the political parties in the 1980s as a way to circumvent election laws and raise huge sums of money that would boost party strength and help elect party candidates, an increasing number of contributors have come to view the soft money system as a means to their own ends. Now the interests on both sides of the system—party fundraisers on the one hand and contributors on the other—have figured out how to exploit the system and one another to their own advantage.

And while these corporate, labor union and individual donors are giving large sums of soft money to promote their own interests, the hundreds of millions of dollars in unregulated money they have poured into the political parties have also had a cumulative effect on the country's political system, analysts say. Their huge contributions are fueling what some campaign finance experts call a political "arms race" and spending war that shows no signs of stopping.

Some observers believe the soft money spiral has corrupted the nation's political system and put the government up for sale. They say the soft money race is fueling a trend toward larger party roles in federal campaigns, blurring the policy differences between the two major parties and, perhaps, generating the growing interest in alternative political parties.

"Federal election law limits individual contributions to $1,000 per candidate per election..."

The Price You Pay for Democracy

When it comes to political contributions, there are several different kinds. Individuals and political action committees (PACs) can give campaign money to congressional and presidential candidates and PACs. Federal election law limits individual contributions to $1,000 per candidate per election; PAC contributions are capped at $5,000 per candidate per election. To distinguish these contributions from soft money donations, they're sometimes referred to as hard money.

Corporations have been barred from making federal campaign contributions since 1904, and in the 1940s Congress extended the ban to labor unions. But the law does allow businesses and unions to make campaign contributions through their PACs, which raise relatively small amounts of money from individual company employees and union members and then give candidates as much as $5,000 per election.

Soft money flies in the face of all contribution restrictions; most of it comes from corporations and unions, and the amounts are unlimited. Because soft money contradicts the spirit, if not the letter, of the law, many contributors don't like to talk about it and try to blur the hard money-soft money distinctions.

Soft money "is sort of an amorphous term anyway," Democratic contributor Michael Caddell says in a typically dismissive comment. "All money is hard when it comes out of your pocket. It's hard to give it away."

That may be, but soft money usually comes in much, much larger amounts than hard money, and the parties are prohibited from using it to campaign directly for their presidential and congressional candidates. The money is supposed to be spent on "party-building" activities, which have come to include everything from rent and staff salaries to get-out-the-vote drives and multimillion-dollar television advertising campaigns that influence federal elections. Parties also channel soft money funds to their state organizations, particularly in states where a presidential race or U.S. Senate election is expected to be close. Soft money also frees up other party funds for use on presidential and congressional campaigns.

Critics charge that the soft money system is nothing more than political money laundering, an operation designed to bring illegal contributions into federal elections. While national party officials say they're raising soft money to promote their party and all its candidates, many soft money donors are giving huge sums to one or both parties with the understanding that their contributions will win them access and influence in Washington. Soft money is raised by federal officials, including the president; donors say they give it to elect party candidates to Congress and the presidency; and the parties spend it in ways that affect federal elections.

More and more, big soft money contributions to the political parties are viewed by corporate executives as the basic club membership fee. And, as more companies want to join the club or feel a need to ante up to the political kitty simply to keep pace with their competitors, the price keeps gong up.

"The whole system has become so dollar-driven," says conservative political analyst Kevin Phillips, "that outfits that haven't participated" in the soft money game before now can't give their money away fast enough. "If you don't pay, you don't play," he says.

But things could be worse, says Robert Buker, senior vice president of United States Sugar Corp., an agribusiness that gives generously to both parties. "You could have absolutely no political problems in a dictatorship," he says.

"It's the price you pay for democracy," Buker says of big political contributions, reflecting at once a prevailing attitude among contributors about the role of corporate cash in the country's political system and an increasingly common equation of democracy with free-market enterprise. It's as if Adam Smith's proverbial invisible hand now holds a fistful of campaign cash.

Buker and many business and union contributors view the multimillion-dollar, bipartisan soft money system as little more than the cost of doing business in a free but regulated marketplace, a price they're happy to pay as long as the system serves them well. "We don't make the rules," says John Sturdivant, president of the American Federation of Government Employees, "we have just learned to use the rules in ways that benefit the people who pay the dues."

But political analyst Phillips looks at the effect of both that attitude and large sums of corporate and labor money on how government operates and sees a huge, fundamental problem. Big money so permeates the political system that "it's corrupt," Phillips says. The government itself has become a marketplace. "It's buy a law, buy a regulation, buy an amendment," he says.

And in the political marketplace, like any other, you get what you pay for, according to Buker.

"I'm not going to be able to see a member [of Congress], generally, unless there is a way to get in. It generally takes contributions," he says, adding that bigger contributions buy better access. Buker should know; since January 1991 his company has contributed $199,050 to the Democratic Party and $31,000 to the Republicans.

"Let's be realistic," says Sturdivant, whose union has given the Democrats $121,074 in soft money since January 1991. "The more contributions you make, the more rooms you get into."

What a $1,500 contribution gets a donor is "not much," according to Buker. "You might get invited to a dinner...with 10,000 other people at it for that kind of money," he says, adding that "$1,500 may buy you 'face time,' so that you can call up a member of the House of Representatives.... The money may allow you to have good access at some levels."

A $50,000 contribution is something else again. "The way you get treated [for that kind of money]," Buker says, "is that if you have a hot issue you can pick up the phone and call the fundraiser and say, 'I need to talk to whoever in the party is making the decision on these issues because I want to give him my point of view.' And you'll get to whoever will make the decision, and you can talk to them and sometimes you'll win and sometimes you'll lose," he adds.

But Buker's not complaining. His company, a beneficiary of a huge government handout program that leaves U.S. consumers paying twice the world price for sugar, wins more often than not.

According to party officials, however, Buker and other big donors are confused about the impact of their contributions. "Maybe they feel they're in a special position," says Democratic National Committee (DNC) spokesperson Amy Weiss Tobe, "but the truth is that they are not getting access.... No one's getting any special access because they're giving money to the DNC."

Republican National Committee (RNC) spokesperson Mary Crawford says her party's soft money donors are invited to meetings—in groups of 200 donors or so—two to four times a year. The private meetings feature "a variety of people" and focus on current policy issues, she says. Told that soft money contributors say their donations buy them access to party and elected officials, Crawford says, "You're welcome to draw whatever conclusions you want. I'm not going to engage in conjecture."

But one big Democratic soft money contributor, a wealthy individual who prefers to remain anonymous, says large contributions are a prerequisite for political influence. "Every [corporate] board I have ever sat on," he says, requires that "you recuse yourself when an issue comes up where you have a vested financial self-interest. The amazing thing about the way business is done in Washington," he says, "is not only do you not recuse yourself, but you'd better get your ass up there and pay everyone you possibly can.

"It's unbelievable, it's incredibly unethical, and it's mind boggling," he continues, "and it makes me really angry." And, he adds in the next breath, "I am going to continue to give money."

Why? "You have to be part of the process," he says. "You have to work inside and outside. If you truly want to be effective as a businessperson you cannot avoid any possible option."

Permanent Interests, Double Givers

For businesses, labor unions, trade groups and others who either have business dealings with the government or whose business dealings are affected by government laws, regulations or broad policies, soft money represents another opportunity to set the agenda and influence the process. Special interest groups like the soft money system precisely because soft money contributions are unregulated and unlimited.

Federal limits on campaign contributions to candidates are the same for all individuals and all PACs. But when it comes to making unregulated contributions to the political parties, the sky's the limit. Huge corporations and wealthy individuals can contribute as much as they want, which is usually far more than smaller companies—not to mention the average voter—can kick in.

"Philip Morris... has given the parties more than $2.7 million in soft money..."

"In the 1994 campaign I 'maxed out' to several" congressional candidates, says a Republican soft money donor, "and I thought that was crazy.... Ultimately, giving to the party was the only way to add dollars to the effort to get those people elected." Like many others, this soft money donor, southern California business owner Darrell Issa, gives his money to promote the election of particular federal candidates—even though soft money contributions go into "non-federal" accounts and are not supposed to be used to aid the election of congressional or presidential candidates.

Other soft money contributions follow the issues of the day. The tobacco industry, for example, has responded to Clinton administration proposals to increase the federal tax on cigarettes and strengthen federal regulation of tobacco products with record-setting contributions to the Republicans. Led by Philip Morris and RJR Nabisco, tobacco interests contributed more than $2.3 million in soft money to the GOP last year, more than four times the amount they gave the party in 1993, and $423,962 to the Democrats, more than double their 1993 contributions.

Those recent contributions put several tobacco companies at or near the top of the list of all soft money contributors for the 1991-95 period. Philip Morris, which has given the parties more than $2.7 million in soft money during that time, is the No. 1 "double donor" and ranks second, just behind Amway, among all soft money contributors. RJR Nabisco, which has contributed more than $2.2 million in soft money, and U.S. Tobacco Co. (UST), with more than $1 million in party contributions, rank third and seventh, respectively, among double donors.

The *Democratic* Club

These are the top 10 soft money contributors to the Democratic Party since January 1991. Where appropriate, executives and subsidiaries are included.

National Education Association	$ 1,132,913
American Federation of State, County and Municipal Employees	$ 996,944
Archer Daniels Midland Co. (ADM)	$ 819,000
Atlantic Richfield Co. (ARCO)	$ 732,648
Laborers' International Union of North America	$ 713,150
Joseph E. Seagram & Sons Inc.	$ 699,614
American Financial Corp.	$ 675,000
Connell Rice & Sugar Co.	$ 659,600
Service Employees International Union	$ 644,675
MCA Inc.	$ 634,003

Long distance and local telephone companies have also substantially upped their soft money giving during key legislative battles. Facing the first major overhaul of telecommunications legislation since 1934, they gave the parties more than $1.4 million in soft money in the last six months of 1995. Long distance giants AT&T, MCI and Sprint gave the parties 4.5 times as much soft money from July through December as they had during the same period in 1994, while the seven Baby Bells increased their soft money contributions by 2.5 times.

The Baby Bells gave Republicans twice as much as Democrats all through 1995, while the long distance carriers made timely contributions to both parties during final negotiations over the legislation. In mid-October, a week before House and Senate conferees began meeting to iron out their differences, MCI gave the Democrats $100,000. On December 21, one day after the conferees reached an agreement that included Clinton administration-supported provisions favorable to the long distance companies, AT&T gave the DNC $ 190,000.

But the House and Senate still had to approve the compromise version, and a week later, after House Republicans had declared the bill "dead as Elvis," AT&T gave the RNC $200,000 in soft money. A day later MCI gave the Democrats another $100,000, along with $20,000 to the GOP.

On February 1, Congress gave final approval to the legislation, which deregulates roughly one-sixth of the nation's economy by removing competitive barriers among local and long distance telephone companies, cable television and broadcasters. President Clinton signed it into law on February 8, and since then the economy has seen a rash of telecommunications mergers.

Was it the holiday spirit or a sudden surge of patriotism that prompted AT&T to make $390,000 in soft money contributions during an eight-day period that included Christmas, or might Ma Bell officials have been hoping to influence congressional conferees with their generosity? Asked to comment, AT&T officials issued the following statement:

"AT&T believes that soft money contributions support the two-party system. The contributions go to state party organizations, and that's a good way to strengthen parties on a state-by-state basis. We also believe that such contributions support strong central parties and, in turn, support democracy."

Other recent issue-related soft money surges include contributions from lawyers battling tort reform; increased giving from health care providers, insurance companies, drug makers and alcohol distributors who support or oppose various aspects of health care reform and proposed changes to Medicare and Medicaid; and labor contributions made in opposition to the NAFTA trade agreement or general Republican policies.

Money also follows money. The National Association of Retail Druggists (NARD), for example, had been making hard money contributions through its PAC for almost 15 years before it joined the soft money club. Since January 1991 it has given $52,949 in soft money to the Democrats. What fueled NARD's entry into the soft money arena? "It put us in play where our opponents were," says John Rector, senior vice president and general counsel of the association.

"The level of soft money fundraising and giving exploded in 1994..."

For a variety of reasons, wealthy special interests are exploiting the soft money loophole like never before. The level of soft money fundraising and giving exploded in 1994, a midterm election year, when the $56.9 million raised almost matched the record-setting total for the presidential election year of 12992. Soft money totals for last year, a non-election year—when all types of political contributions usually decline dramatically—increased by 4 percent to almost $59.4 million. And that was more than double the amount raised in 1993, the previous non-election year.

The *Republican* Club

These are the top 10 soft money donors to the Republican Party since January 1991. Their totals include contributions from executives and subsidiaries.

Amway Corp.	$	2,810,000
Philip Morris Co. Inc.	$	2,291,776
Archer Daniels Midland Co.	$	1,682,268
RJR Nabisco	$	1,626,757
American Financial Corp.	$	1,475,000
Atlantic Richfield Co. (ARCO)	$	1,336,113
Merrill Lynch & Co. Inc.	$	925,700
U.S. Tobacco Co.	$	865,466
Joseph E. Seagram & Sons Inc.	$	724,727
Chevron Corp.	$	708,422

Mixed Doubles

Here are the top 10 donors to both parties since January 1991. Their contribution totals include donations from executives and company subsidiaries.

	TO DEMOCRATS	TO REPUBLICANS	TOTAL
Philip Morris	$ 453,500	$ 2,291,776	$ 2,745,276
Archer Daniels Midland Co. (ADM)	$ 819,000	$ 1,682,268	$ 2,501,268
RJR Nabisco	$ 579,900	$ 1,626,757	$ 2,206,757
American Financial Corp.	$ 675,000	$ 1,475,000	$ 2,150,000
Atlantic Richfield Co. (ARCO)	$ 732,648	$ 1,336,113	$ 2,068,761
Joseph E. Seagram & Sons Inc.	$ 699,614	$ 724,727	$ 1,424,341
U.S. Tobacco Co.	$ 201,308	$ 865,466	$ 1,066,774
Merrill Lynch & Co. Inc.	$ 139,300	$ 925,700	$ 1,065,000
Chevron Corp.	$ 347,838	$ 708,422	$ 1,056,260
MCI Telecommunications Corp.	$ 569,214	$ 371,870	$ 941,084

"Some 254 soft money contributors have given at least $20,000 to both parties..."

But it's more than soft money grand totals that are on the increase. More corporations, unions and individuals are giving soft money, and—in what is perhaps the most significant development of all—more of them are making large contributions to not just one, but both political parties.

"The world has changed, and we must too," says Melinda Anderson, spokesperson for the National Education Association (NEA), explaining why the nation's largest teachers' union—and No. 1 soft money contributor to the Democratic Party since 1991—has started giving soft money to the GOP. "We will continue to contribute on the Democratic side of the aisle," she says, but "this year we have reached out significantly to the Republican side." Earlier this year the union bought tables at fundraising dinners for the Republican Senatorial Campaign Committee and the Republican governors association, she says.

"In American politics, one side or the other is never permanently on top," says U.S. Sugar's Buker. "You just see the Congress changing hands; you see the White House changing hands. If you become an enemy of one side or another, you'll find out that you don't have very good access when they come in power," he adds.

"There are no permanent friends, no permanent enemies. There are just permanent interests," explains the government employees union's Sturdivant.

An analysis of records filed with the Federal Election Commission (FEC) confirms the observation: Both the Republican and Democratic parties are now largely corporation-funded and, to a great extent, by the *same* corporations. Some 254 soft money contributors have given at least $20,000 to both parties since January 1991, and 132 of those donors have contributed at least

$50,000 to both parties. Fifty-nine double donors have given each party at least $100,000. Andreas's Archer Daniels Midland Co., oil conglomerate ARCO, Lindner's American Financial Corp. empire, and alcohol giant Joseph E. Seagram & Sons Inc. make each party's list of top 10 soft money givers.

This suggests that, more than ever before, soft money contributions are given to gain access and influence and set the political agenda. And as the number of donors making huge contributions to both political parties increases, some analysts believe the policy differences between the parties have begun to decrease.

"The two parties have become much more similar in their basic policy approaches because they both have similar [financial] bases now," says Tony Corrado, a professor of government at Colby College who's writing a book on how the parties get and spend their money. "There is an increasingly narrow gap between the two parties when you put all the issues on the table.

"Sure, more labor money goes to Democrats," he continues, "but there aren't that many differences in the types of big donors to each party. It's not like one is the corporate party and one is the individual party."

Look for the Union Label

While soft money contributions from corporations and business interests outweigh labor union contributions by roughly 12-to-1, labor money continues to stand out for the role it plays in the Democratic Party. Roughly 99 percent of labor's soft money goes to the Democrats, and two of the top four and four of the top 10 Democratic soft money contributors are unions. Yet when it comes to total dollar amounts contributed to the Democrats, business interests still outspend unions by an 8-to-1 ratio.

"For decades the Democratic Party was our vehicle for moving our agenda," says the NEA's Anderson. And although 1.1 million NEA dollars made the union the Democrats' top soft money contributor from 1991-95, Anderson says the NEA' s membership has decided to be more bipartisan.

"Our members have said over and over that they want us to be less partisan and more issue-driven," she says, adding that that means looking for Republican congressmembers who share the union's views as well as making political contributions to Republican Party committees. This summer the NEA will also attempt, for the first time, to participate in the platform debate at the Republicans' national convention, she adds.

But the AFL-CIO has already endorsed President Clinton's reelection bid, and most other unions and labor dollars will stay with the Democrats. And the union's announcement that it plans to raise and spend $35 million on a largely anti-Republican advertising campaign and grassroots organizing effort has Republican leaders and think-tank allies plotting retaliatory measures.

"This is not about whether labor is going to be a mainstay of the Democratic Party," says John Sturdivant of the American Federation of Government Employees (AFGE), "this is about what kind of country we are going to have. There are fundamental differences between this president and this Congress."

On the NAFTA trade agreement and health care reform, however, the unions suffered major defeats at the hands of both the president and the formerly Democratic Congress. But the unions do have the support of Clinton and many Democratic congressmembers in their efforts to raise the minimum wage, minimize planned cuts in Medicare spending, and block corporate and Republican efforts to weaken workplace safety laws.

And in revising the Hatch Act early in his term, Clinton effectively opened the door to even larger labor PAC contributions. A key revision allows federal and postal employee unions to set up payroll deduction plans to collect members' PAC contributions.

"...unions seem to have become more pragmatic about their political giving..."

If anything, unions seem to have become more pragmatic about their political giving, which is in part a reaction to the feeling among many labor leaders that Democrats have taken their support for granted. William Luddy, political director of the United Brotherhood of Carpenters and Joiners, which has given $146,575 to the Democratic Party since early 1991, says his union is reassessing how it makes political contributions, and to whom.

"This is a tough business," says AFGE's Sturdivant. "In this business the only reason why people deal with you is if they think you can help them or they think you can hurt them."

Sturdivant, whose union has about 210,000 dues-paying members, says Democratic leaders looking for contributions got the cold shoulder from AFGE after President Clinton proposed a pay freeze for government workers early in his term. "We told them they were going to get the minimum level, and the only reason they were going to get the minimum level was because it got us in the room to give them hell," he says, adding, "and I got my money's worth."

Dan Lucas, political director of the Service Employees International Union (SEIU), says he has talked about union concerns with Clinton White House and Cabinet officials on several occasions. Officials at SEIU, which has given the Democrats $644,675 in soft money since January 1991, "have never had a problem meeting with anyone we wanted to meet with," Lucas says.

Vincent Panvini, director of government affairs for the Sheet Metal Workers Association, which gave the Democrats $432,000 during the period, says "there are a lot more open doors [in the Clinton administration] than you had during Reagan and Bush."

But even as labor unions increase their political activity and enjoy broad access to Clinton administration officials, some observers believe the federal government continues to adopt more pro-business policies. In addition to the $100 billion in subsidies, tax breaks, loans and promotions—often called corporate welfare—the government doles out to business every year, the

Clinton administration provided high-profile support for the NAFTA and GATT trade agreements and has served as a marketing agent for huge multinational corporations, many of them soft money donors, on taxpayer-financed global "trade missions" that have resulted in more than $20 billion in private business deals. The Clinton White House has also invited CEOs and business representatives, many of them soft money donors, to participate in its discussions and formulations of public policy.

Take, for example, the president's Council on Sustainable Development. Created by Clinton in 1993, the 24-person panel was charged with formulating a plan that would promote economic growth while protecting natural resources. Clinton appointed the members, four of whom are administration officials. Of the remaining 20, nine are top executives of leading corporations—including Enron Corp., the world's largest natural gas company; General Motors Corp., the nation's biggest car manufacturer; Chevron Corp., a huge oil company; and Georgia-Pacific Corp., a top logging company. Also on the council is a top official of the AFL-CIO, the country's largest union.

The council is co-chaired by a vice president of Dow Chemical Co., one of the country's largest producers of dioxins. The union and all of the nine corporations or their representatives—or both—have made large soft money contributions to the political parties; six of the nine have contributed to both parties.

First, Kill the Anti-Lawyer Bills

Trial lawyers and law firms are another group of large soft money donors that has fared well under the Clinton administration. President Clinton has sided with the lawyers on all their key issues—opposition to reforms of securities, product liability and malpractice laws—even though that has meant vetoing two popular bills and incurring the wrath of some top congressional Democrats.

It's no secret that trial lawyers have long favored Democrats. In his acceptance speech at the Republican National Convention in 1992, then-President Bush snarled that Bill Clinton was backed "by every trial lawyer who ever wore a tasseled loafer," and, for all its hyperbole, the statement was almost accurate. As a group, lawyers were the single biggest contributor to Clinton's '92 campaign, giving almost $3 million in hard dollars. And lawyers are right on track to give as much or more to his reelection bid; in the first nine months of '95 they contributed $2.5 million to the Clinton-Gore campaign, according to the Center for Responsive Politics.

Lawyers are also a mainstay in Democratic Party fundraising circles. Since 1991 attorneys and law firms have given the Democrats more than $7 million in soft money. So when Clinton vetoed legal reform bills, many observers said he had caved in to high-powered, big-giving trial lawyers.

Last December Clinton vetoed a bill that supporters said would have protected corporations from many investor lawsuits. Among the bill's strongest backers were many Silicon Valley high-tech computer firms, whose executives had provided critical business support to Clinton's '92 campaign. Securities fraud lawsuits have become such a problem for these firms that they reportedly spent more than $12 million on advertising campaigns to support three legal reform initiatives on California's March primary ballot. But they lost to the trial lawyers there as well.

White House aides said Clinton largely favored the securities lawsuit bill and agonized over it before he finally vetoed it for two specific provisions. But the bill's supporters credited the political pull of San Diego trial lawyer William Lerach for the presidential quash. An aide to Rep. Thomas Bliley (R-Va.) told the *Washington Post* that Clinton's veto was "a payoff to a major fat-cat trial lawyer," meaning Lerach.

"Clinton's veto of the securities fraud bill also put him at odds with some members of his own party..."

But Lerach told the *Post* he hadn't spoken to the president about the legislation, saying his views on the matter are so well known that he didn't need to. Indeed, in corporate investment circles Lerach is known as the "king" of shareholder suits, and in Democratic fundraising circles he's known for his deep pockets. A contributor of $382,500 in soft money to Democratic committees since 1991, Lerach is no stranger to the White House, either. In 1994 he attended a state dinner for the president of Ukraine, and last December, just a few days before Clinton vetoed the securities lawsuits bill, Lerach attended a White House event for Democratic fundraisers. Melvyn Weiss, one of Lerach's law firm partners, has contributed $190,000 to the Democrats; Lerach's firm ranks 11th on the list of top Democratic soft money givers. Lerach did not respond to interview requests.

Lee Godfrey, a Houston-based titan of securities lawsuits, has given the Democrats $72,300 in soft money and raised thousands more. Last December, when it was time for the president to file for reelection in Texas, it was Godfrey who submitted the paperwork.

Clinton's veto of the securities fraud bill also put him at odds with some members of his own party, who joined with Republicans in both houses to override the veto. And by March some Democrats had joined the chorus of complaints about the political influence of trial lawyers. Sen. Jay Rockefeller (D-W.Va.) said the president's intention to veto a bill designed to limit lawsuits over faulty products was motivated by "special interests and raw political considerations."

In fact, the nation's top product liability and class action lawyers are also big Democratic donors. On February 29, three weeks before the Senate passed the product liability reform bill, the Association of Trial Lawyers of America (ATLA) gave the Democrats $100,000, according to the Associated Press. That's on top of the $166,000 ATLA gave the Democrats from 1991-95. Clinton vetoed the bill May 2. And the Cincinnati law firm of Stanley Chesley, considered the "godfather" of class actions on everything from Agent Orange and asbestos exposure to breast implants and defective heart valves, has contributed $307,000 to the Democrats since 1991—a small investment for a firm that's been known to win more than $10 million for a single case.

So legendary is the power of the trial lawyers on the issue that even though product liability reform legislation has been around for some 13 years, this was the first bill to make it through Congress and to a president's desk—despite the lobbying, financial and political support of a whole array of corporate, insurance and business interests who've given tens of millions of soft money dollars to both parties. "This is not David versus Goliath," said Sen. Joseph Lieberman (D-Conn.), a key tort reform supporter. "This is two Goliaths battling each other."

But to Senate Majority Leader and presumptive Republican presidential nominee Bob Dole, the villain was clear. "If money talks," he said, "this money screams."

How Sweet It Is

Dole should know, say some observers, who accuse him of being a good money listener. In the Washington world of code-speak, where the most important message delivered in a public speech often fails to make the headlines, Dole's statement at a March 21 press conference was a classic wink-and-nod performance.

The story about the $47 billion farm bill in the next day's *Washington Post* mentioned a Florida Everglades cleanup provision as "a high-profile item for Republicans eager to demonstrate the GOP's friendliness to the environment," and quoted Dole's description of the measure as "an indication that we're serious about this." Another reporter noted Dole's not-so-subtle jab at the Clinton administration's approach to the problem, in which Dole remarked that his party could clean up the environment without raising taxes.

Few listeners caught the true meaning of Dole's remarks, which were tailor-made, as was the provision, for his supporters in the south Florida sugar industry. The $200 million Everglades restoration plan, which also authorizes the expenditure of another $100 million to be gained from selling or swapping federal land, spares the sugar growers—whose fertilizer-rich runoff has wreaked havoc in the unique ecosystem—of additional financial responsibility for the cleanup. Instead it spreads the cost among all U.S. taxpayers, most of whom have never seen the Everglades.

Dole, House Speaker Newt Gingrich, Florida Sens. Connie Mack (R) and Bob Graham (D) and Rep. Mark Foley (R-Fla.) were particularly pleased with the resolution of the Everglades issue because they had essentially pulled victory from the jaws of defeat for the sugar growers. Some of the region's most powerful sugar producers are also key supporters of the Republican Party and Dole's presidential campaign.

From all previous indications, this was going to be the year in which the highly subsidized sugar industry was forced to take its lumps. A powerful senator, the White House and a broad-based Florida environmental coalition bankrolled by a New York multi-millionaire were all calling for a special assessment on sugar growers to finance an effort to restore some ecological balance to the Everglades marshlands. A public opinion poll showed that two-thirds of Florida residents supported the idea.

Sen. Richard Lugar (R-Ind.), who had been trying to eliminate what he calls the sugar industry's "federally guaranteed monopoly profit" for almost 20 years, was now chair of the Senate Agriculture Committee. According to the U.S. General Accounting Office (GAO), federal sugar price supports cost Americans $1.4 billion a year in higher sugar, candy, food and soft drink prices—or a price fully double the going rate on the world market. Government trade policies inflate U.S. sugar prices by controlling sugar imports; the industry also benefits from federally subsidized water projects.

Lugar introduced legislation calling for a two cents-per-pound assessment on all sugar cane produced in the Everglades area, a levy he estimated would generate $350 million over five years, to buy sugar land in the region and take it out of production. In fact, Lugar's proposed "assessment" would have simply reduced by two cents the 18 cents-a-pound subsidy south Florida sugar growers receive from the federal government. "As the longtime beneficiary of a severely misguided big-government program," Lugar said, "the Florida sugar industry has contributed to the problem and must take primary responsibility for solving it."

In February Vice President Al Gore traveled to south Florida to announce a $1.5 billion Everglades restoration program, which would have been funded in part by a penny-a-pound sugar "assessment."

"But Dole was on the opposite side of the issue," along with Mack and Graham, says Lugar spokesperson Andy Fisher. "They had the idea of taking money out of the general fund in the farm bill." Sure enough, the Everglades provision showed up in the bill's final version.

The sugar industry came out a double winner. The Dole-endorsed Everglades plan let growers off the hook, and the $47 billion farm bill—which phases out government subsidies to growers of corn, cotton, rice and wheat and producers of butter, powdered milk and cheese—left intact the price-support system for sugar cane growers.

The region's sugar producers, who have long made their wishes known to Washington lawmakers with a powerful combination of soft money, PAC contributions, well-heeled lobbyists and close relationships with Dole and other key officials, had vociferously opposed both the Clinton and Lugar proposals.

"They are very aggressive," Fisher says.

U.S. Sugar's Buker complains in an interview that multi-millionaire Paul Tudor Jones II and Florida environmentalists are "attacking" the industry. Referring to the 1994 settlement of a federal lawsuit that requires the growers to pay up to $320 million in cleanup costs over 20 years, Buker says the industry is already doing its part.

The proposed reductions in the federal sugar subsidy would drive his company and other growers out of business, says Buker, who is just as blunt in his discussion of the big soft money contributions his company has made to both political parties. "It's to protect our business interests," he says. "You give it so you can get access."

And, Buker adds, echoing a refrain common among big soft money contributors, "We run up against a ton more money on the other side."

In fact, some of the sugar industry's more traditional opponents, including soft drink and candy makers, are also big soft money givers. Coca-Cola has contributed $333,983 to the Republicans since January 1991, along with $117,203 to the Democrats; PepsiCo Inc. has given the Republicans $267,474; and Mars Inc. has contributed $136,000 to the GOP.

Jones, meanwhile, the New York commodity trader who financed an expensive advertising campaign in support of an Everglades cleanup tax on the sugar growers, has contributed $190,000 to the Democrats. Despite all his political contributions and millions spent on advertising, ballot initiatives and grassroots organizing, Jones discovered that he couldn't beat Big Sugar. At least not yet.

This is at least in part, many believe, because of a couple of brothers: Jose "Pepe" and Alfonso Fanjul of Palm Beach, the owners of Flo-Sun Sugar Co. Inc., the most dominant grower in Florida's sugar industry, and Okeelanta Corp., its sugar mill. Flo-Sun has contributed $30,000 to the Republicans since January 1991 (on top of Jose's $200,000 gift to the RNC as a member of President Bush's Team 100) and $21,000 to the Democrats, while Okeelanta has given the Republicans $159,500 and the Democrats $53,000.

Never mind that the brothers are not U.S. citizens and therefore cannot vote; as Cuban exiles with Spanish passports and permanent U.S. resident status they're far more involved in American politics than most citizens will ever be.

Jose "Pepe" Fanjul also has strong personal ties to high-ranking Republican officials. Fanjul was a fundraiser for George Bush in 1988 and a finance committee vice chair for Bush's 1992 campaign. He is now a vice chair of Bob Dole's national finance committee; last year he hosted a fundraiser for Dole at his Palm Beach estate that netted more than $100,000.

Alfonso Fanjul, meanwhile, was a top fundraiser for Bill Clinton's 1992 campaign.

Farmworkers' rights advocates have blamed the Fanjuls' ties to top Republican leaders, including Bush Commerce Secretary Robert Mosbacher, for the Labor Department's repeated failure in the late 1980s to crack down on Fanjul companies for labor-law violations involving the abuse of Caribbean sugar cane cutters.

Many observers believe the Fanjuls' connections and contributions also had a lot to do with the Everglades provision that ended up in the farm bill. Representatives of the Fanjuls did not respond to repeated requests for interviews.

Others believe Dole's Everglades plan had more to do with election-year politics than the powerful sugar industry. With Florida's 25 electoral votes a coveted prize on Election Night, Dole was bound to produce a pro-Everglades plan of his own once the White House announced its proposal, they say.

Dole provided support for that view in early April when, while vacationing at his Florida condo (sold to Elizabeth Dole by long-time supporter and leading double-soft money donor Dwayne Andreas), Dole took time out to plug the Everglades plan. After a helicopter ride over the Everglades with West Palm Beach's Rep. Foley, Dole voiced support for the cleanup and reiterated his opposition to Clinton's proposed penny-a-pound sugar tax. "You can't pick out a single industry," Dole said.

However, a Dole spokesperson insists the senator's support for a farm bill Everglades provision had nothing to do with either campaign activities or his ties to the sugar industry. "Sen. Dole has been guided by the 10th Amendment, which is to return power to the states," says Clarkson Hine. "His view is that people in Florida can decide on this issue, not people in Washington."

Asked how a provision in a federal farm bill empowers state residents, Hine says, "The federal government helps start the state effort, and now the people of Florida have the opportunity to decide how best to proceed." Whatever the reason the Everglades plan won Dole's endorsement, the real winners are the sugar producers.

The Drug Lords

Much of the Washington business that soft money donors care about most happens not in Congress or a White House office, but at the regulatory level, where political appointees and bureaucrats enforce the law, conduct inspections and investigations, file lawsuits and approve products. Many of the rooms soft money donors speak of gaining access to are the offices of top regulators and administrators—persons who are not elected but who wield a lot of power over the way businesses operate and the profits they can earn.

So in late March, when news was leaked of a Federal Trade Commission (FTC) investigation into the pricing policies of 22 major pharmaceutical firms, officials at the trade group representing drug stores considered the development a major political victory. The National Association of Retail Druggists (NARD) had been asking the FTC to investigate the drug makers since 1982, says NARD general counsel John Rector. Written requests from

Democratic Reps. John Dingell and Jack Brooks in the mid-1980s also had failed to prompt FTC action.

NARD accuses the drug companies of conspiring to charge drugstores higher prices for prescription drugs while offering bulk discounts to hospitals and HMOs. In February, 15 drug companies agreed to pay more than $400 million to settle a class action lawsuit, and in May, 13 of them agreed to stop charging pharmacies higher prices.

The drug companies and their trade group, the Pharmaceutical Research and Manufacturers Association (PRMA), are renowned for their political clout—and their campaign contributions. Rector and his association members believed the FTC's refusal to investigate the drug companies for possible price-fixing or other anti-competitive behavior was a function of the drug makers' influence and the free-market philosophy of some Reagan and Bush appointees. An FTC spokesperson refused to comment on the current probe.

"From January 1991 through 1995 NARD gave the DNC $52,949 in soft money..."

Rector relates his experience at a Washington social gathering in the mid-'80s shortly after Rep. Brooks had written FTC commissioners requesting an investigation. Representatives of the drug makers' trade group, then called the PMA, were also at the party, and Rector says he overheard them "boasting" about the FTC's response to Brooks. It turned out that while Brooks had yet to hear from the FTC, PMA officials had a draft copy of the FTC's response.

"We used to say that the PMA and the FTC had the same phone number," Rector says.

So in the late 1980s NARD started supplementing its PAC contributions with soft money. "It gave us access to circumstances that could be beneficial," Rector says, explaining that "drug companies are everywhere at political conventions. A lot of times you can't even participate in activities" that provide access to convention delegates—who are often congressmembers, governors and other elected officials—without making big contributions to the parties, Rector says. "A little went a long way," he adds. From January 1991 through 1995 NARD gave the DNC $52,949 in soft money; last year it also gave $3,500 to the RNC.

Asked about PRMA's contributions to the political parties, spokesperson Patrick Korten first says, "We don't give soft money." When informed that the association has given $70,987 in soft money to the Republicans and $49,950 to the Democrats since 1991, Korten says, "We're no different than any other association in town. We buy tickets to [party] dinners. Whether it's PAC contributions or soft money dinner tickets," he adds, "we are in no way, shape or form a big player in this business."

PRMA's member companies, however, have contributed more than $3.8 million in soft money since January 1991.

Hard and soft political contributions are only part of NARD's strategy. "We've left no stone unturned," Rector says. In fact, shortly after Clinton was elected—before he'd even taken office—Rector met with and wrote a memo to members of Clinton's FTC transition team, outlining his group's concerns and expressing his "hope that the new FTC will provide leadership essential to achieve these objectives."

In Rector's view the money, the lobbying and the schmoozing are all necessary to help retail druggists "level what [their] opponents can give.... If every issue were argued on the merits and won on the merits, that would be great," he says. "Unfortunately, our system is not set up that way."

A History of Favors

While party officials, members of Congress and most soft money contributors insist that contributions are given to parties or candidates who already support a contributor's position on key issues, contributions from one donor to both parties beg the question: Do big soft money contributions follow sympathetic parties and candidates, or are huge sums of money given to gain access to administration officials and congressmembers in the hopes of gaining their support? In other words, do votes, vetoes, regulations, policies and other government actions sometimes follow the money? While direct quid pro quos are inherently difficult to prove, presidential, congressional and regulatory actions that are favorable to large donors suggest that money can pervert the process.

When Clinton administration officials, Senate Majority Leader Dole, House Speaker Gingrich and House Minority Leader Dick Gephardt pulled out all the stops earlier this year to try to stop trade quotas limiting imports of Chiquita brand bananas, many observers suspected political money was at play. How often does that grouping of individuals agree on anything, they reasoned. And Chiquita owner Carl Lindner and his American Financial Corp. and various subsidiaries have given the political parties more than $2.1 million since January 1991, with almost $1.5 million of that going to the Republicans. Lindner had also contributed $100,000 to Dole's now defunct tax-exempt foundation and at least $55,000 to GOPAC, the controversial political group formerly headed by Gingrich.

As a Lindner aide said of his boss, "He needs help this year.... That's what the Congress and the administration are there for." And he got it, with the top leaders of both parties pressuring the European Union, Colombia and Costa Rica to take actions benefitting a Lindner-owned company that has almost no American employees.

Leaders of both parties have also gone to bat consistently for ADM, the agribusiness giant owned by longtime political donor Dwayne Andreas. Since January 1991 Andreas, his wife and his company have given the political parties more than $2.5 million in soft money; ADM's almost $1.7 million in GOP contributions make it the No. 3 Republican giver for the period.

In 1994 Vice President Gore cast a tie-breaking Senate vote that favored producers of ethanol, a corn-based fuel additive, over oil companies At the time ADM controlled more than half the ethanol market. Gore's vote killed an effort to prevent the enforcement of a pro-ethanol Environmental Protection Agency (EPA) ruling authorized by the Clinton administration.

That Clean Air Act regulation, which required that roughly 10 percent of all gasoline contain ethanol by January 1995, followed reports by the Clinton administration's own Energy Department that ethanol might actually cause more pollution and be more expensive than an additive derived from natural gas.

Another president had paved the way for the EPA ruling. In 1992, a month before the presidential election, George Bush announced in a Rose Garden ceremony that he was granting an ethanol exemption to the Clean Air Act's volatility standards. The exemption was necessary because the EPA had determined that ethanol's high volatility meant it would worsen, rather than improve, gasoline pollution during the summer.

"In May 1995 a U.S. Appeals Court struck down the Clinton administration's ethanol mandate..."

The oil industry, environmentalists and some senators criticized the pro-ethanol actions of both administrations as political moves designed to benefit Andreas and win votes in farm states. In 1994 Clinton administration officials said the ethanol requirement would bring farmers an additional $250 million a year, and Dole, sometimes called "Senator Ethanol," was the key leader in the Senate battle to keep the regulation alive.

When the American Petroleum Institute and the National Petroleum Refiners Association filed suit in federal court to block enforcement of the rule, they characterized the ethanol mandate as "the product of special interest politics," and said it would result in the transfer of hundreds of millions of taxpayer dollars to ADM. In May 1995 a U.S. Appeals Court struck down the Clinton administration's ethanol mandate, saying the EPA had exceeded its authority.

But that didn't stop the Clinton administration from trying to help ethanol producers in other ways. Last summer the Treasury Department expanded the ethanol tax subsidy—which, at 54 cents a gallon, costs taxpayers about $770 million a year—to cover ETBE, an ether derived from ethanol. And when Rep. Bill Archer (R-Texas) tried last year to reduce the subsidy by three cents a gallon, Dole and Agriculture Secretary Dan Glickman led the successful fight to preserve the full subsidy.

ADM also benefits from other government subsidies and policies. Federal sugar subsidies boost ADM's sales of high-fructose corn syrup for use in soft drinks, and the company has won more than $68 million in federal "export enhancement" awards in the past three fiscal years alone.

ADM has not fared so well, however, with the Clinton Justice Department, which has been investigating the company for possible price-fixing on three of its products: the soft-drink sweetener; citric acid, also used in soft drinks; and lysine, which is added to animal feed. In April ADM agreed to pay $25 million to settle civil suits that accused ADM and other lysine producers of conspiring to fix prices.

In addition to living in a condo formerly owned by Andreas, Dole is a frequent flyer on ADM's corporate jet. Andreas, like Lindner, contributed $100,000 to Dole's foundation, and in June 1995 both Andreas and his wife, Inez, made the maximum $1,000 contributions to Clinton's legal defense fund.

But the history of government actions taken on behalf of top contributors is nothing new; nor is it limited to the likes of Lindner and Andreas. Previous investigations by *Common Cause Magazine* uncovered a clear pattern of favorable government treatment of big Republican Party donors.

A 1990 investigation ("All the President's Donors," March/April) identified the 249 individuals who had contributed $100,000 each to Team 100, a special big-money drive run out of the Republican National Committee (RNC) to help elect George Bush.

Team 100 was a virtual Who's Who of American business: Sixty-six contributors worked in finance, 58 in real estate and construction, 17 in the oil industry and 15 in food and agriculture. Entertainment, cable television, insurance, steel and auto industries were also represented.

Almost all Team 100 members or the companies they led wanted something from the government, and many of them had significant business or regulatory matters pending with the federal government at the time they made their contributions. Others gave their $100,000 knowing they probably would have business matters come before the Bush administration.

The Democrats had mounted a similar fundraising drive. Together, the parties injected more than $45 million in large individual and corporate contributions into the 1988 presidential race. After the election Team 100 captain Robert Mosbacher was appointed Commerce secretary and six Team 100 members were nominated as U.S. ambassadors.

In 1992, with the Bush administration in its fourth year and the president running for reelection, the magazine revisited Team 100 and uncovered a clear pattern of favorable government treatment of the GOP's $100,000 donors (see "Bush's Ruling Class," April/May/June 1992). The results produced or fostered by their influence included questionable actions, policy reversals, pork barrel handouts, import-export assistance, high-level intervention on regulatory matters, appointments to ambassadorships and federal commissions, and broad national policies for wealthy Wall Street, oil, real estate, cable TV and other interests.

Specific federal actions benefitting Team 100 members included clean air provisions sought by oil, natural gas and ethanol producers; a timely release of federally subsidized irrigation water in California's Central Valley; a $35 million federal grant for construction of a Denver air terminal; the imposition of cement tariffs for the first time in 26 years; and the quashing of a $50 million criminal tax investigation.

According to the RNC's Crawford, Team 100 is still alive and well, representing the top echelon of GOP donors.

As long as Bush was in the White House, the lion's share of six-figure soft money contributions continued to flow to the Republicans. But beginning in mid-1992 and continuing through the first 15 months of Clinton's term, the soft money flow shifted dramatically to the new party in power. Labor unions, the tobacco industry, health care interests, breweries, Wall Streeters and movie moguls were among the interests ponying up to the Democratic soft money trough.

In 1994, however, the flow changed direction again; although contributions to both parties increased, the Republicans collected 55 percent more soft money than the Democrats. Republican Party committees raised $33.9 million last year, more than three times the amount they raised in 1993, the last non-election year. The Democratic Party raised $25.4 million in soft money last year, a 44 percent increase over its '93 total.

It's no wonder that Trevor Potter, a former FEC chair and, before that, a lawyer for the Bush-Quayle campaign finance committee, likens the soft money system to a political "arms race. There is no logical stopping point," he says. Like military superpowers being pressed to disarm, party officials defend their use of soft money by saying, "'We don't want to be caught defenseless. The other party is doing it,'" Potter adds.

"It's kind of like warfare," agrees Lawrence O'Brien III, a lobbyist for telecommunications interests who's contributed $117,750 to the Democrats since January 1991. "It's a balance of power," he says.

Indeed, the soft money fundraising machines of both parties have thrived during the Clinton administration despite the president's repeated statements in support of campaign finance reform.

Same as It Ever Was—Only Worse

It wasn't supposed to be this way. Clinton had campaigned on a platform of change, and he talked repeatedly about changing the way business is done in Washington. Yet even before he took office the president-elect was reaching out to big business, asking corporations to fund numerous inaugural festivities.

President Clinton continued to sound the reform theme in speeches, interviews and radio addresses. "And so I say to all of you here," he said in his inaugural address, "let us resolve to reform our politics so that power and privilege no longer shut down the voice of the people. Let us give this capital back to the people to whom it belongs."

The new president also seemed to understand the impact of big political money on policy. In his first week in office he told *Newsweek*, "It's going to be difficult for us to pass the kind of health care reforms we need, and the kinds of budgetary changes we need, unless we can pass campaign finance and lobby reform."

While Senate Democratic leaders and public interest groups urged the new president to introduce a campaign reform measure almost immediately upon taking office, House Democratic leaders had other ideas. They argued for dealing with other issues first, and for letting them decide when to introduce campaign reform. The House Democrats seemed to win out; while Clinton continued to talk reform, he did nothing about it. Instead, Democratic party leaders actively sought both PAC money and big soft money contributions.

In a May 1993 radio address from the Oval Office, Clinton said, "Unless we change fundamentally the way campaigns are financed, everything else we seek to do to improve the lives of our people will be much harder to achieve. Economic reform and reform of the political system go hand in hand."

"...Democratic party leaders actively sought both PAC money and big soft money contributions."

Clinton criticized lobbyists and special interests for attacking his health reform plan, and said, "This is what always happens in Washington. Narrow interests exercise powerful influence. They try to stop reform, delay change, deny progress, simply because they profit from the status quo. Because big money and the special access it buys are the problem, we have to reform the political system even as we try to improve the economy and open opportunities to all our people."

Senate Democrats managed to pass a strong campaign finance reform measure that month, but away from the public eye party officials were busy raising money. Within days of Clinton's radio speech deploring access-selling, the DNC was banking the more than $3.5 million it had raised at a dinner attended by the president at New York's Lincoln Center. Later that month U.S. Trade Representative Mickey Kantor hosted a private briefing on trade matters for a dozen big-money contributors to the Democratic Party.

"Not only is this business as usual," a former party fundraiser told the *New York Times*, "but they've gone a step beyond."

And they went further still. During that same week in May 1993 the DNC sent out invitations to events that were to include breakfast with the president, private briefings with top-level officials and a lavish dinner party at the Washington Convention Center—all for $15,000 a couple. The invitation made it clear that contributions from PACs and corporations were welcome. After details of the planned event became public and attracted significant criticism, Democratic officials canceled the presidential breakfast.

They could afford to. During Clinton's first 15 months in office, the Democrats raised more than $20.5 million in soft money contributions—50 percent more than the Republicans had raised during the first 15 months of Bush's presidency. And the money was coming from many of the same wealthy individuals and corporations that had filled the GOP's soft money coffers.

The Republicans, meanwhile, were overhauling their money-raising operations and gearing up for the midterm congressional elections in November 1994. In one of the more ironic fundraising perk offers, the GOP attempted to lure its donors to an April '94 fundraiser in New York City. For a $100,000 contribution, donors would be wined and dined by top party officials and attend a political briefing, complete with a "private photo opportunity" with former President Richard Nixon, someone who could talk firsthand about political money scandals.

The Democrats were working on their own hard sell, and in mid-1995 they issued another brazen dining-for-dollars invitation. For $100,000, donors could get not one, but two, dinners with the president, according to a DNC brochure. Meetings with First Lady Hillary Rodham Clinton and Vice President Gore were also part of the package. After more negative publicity, Clinton canceled the dinner dates, but party officials pledged to continue their access-for-sale fundraising methods. "The president was mad about it and said, 'Don't do that,' but we're going to continue to raise money. Those are the facts of life," White House press secretary Mike McCurry told reporters last July.

Some of the GOP's soft money came from similar "access-selling" appeals. Individual contributions of $15,000, and special "rates" of $20,000 per couple and $7,500 for donors under age 35, would bring meetings with top Republican officials, participation in trade missions, preferential seating at the party's national convention and private meetings with the new president and vice president, should the Republicans recapture the White House.

Meanwhile, efforts to reform the campaign financing system continued to languish. House Democrats, who had delayed action for months, finally agreed to a compromise reform package in September 1994, but it was killed by a Republican-led Senate filibuster. Attempts by the president and Democratic leaders to blame the failure on Republicans rang somewhat hollow.

By that time another Election Day was right around the corner, and Rep. Newt Gingrich had engineered a plan for a Republican takeover of the House. A key part of the plan was money. Because most PAC contributions go to incumbents, and because Democrats had controlled the House for 40 years, the lion's share of PAC money had long gone to Democrats. But Gingrich aimed to reverse that trend—even before his party won a majority of House seats.

If PACs often made contributions to ensure access to lawmakers, Gingrich suggested the converse could also be true. "Don't pick a specific (race) out," he told PAC directors attending a Republican Party briefing about a month before the election, "just put your money in any or all of them, because when I become speaker, for anybody that's not on board now it's going to be the coldest two years in Washington." Gingrich's statement also demonstrated how lawmakers often shake down contributors.

In the closing days of the '94 elections, both PACs and big soft money donors rushed to the Republicans. GOP committees collected a record $10.8 million in soft money from October 20 through November 28, three weeks after the election. Among the party's biggest soft-money contributors were tobacco, alcohol and gambling interests.

From January 1993 through November 28, 1994, the Republicans collected $43.9 million in soft money while the Democrats took in $39.4 million.

But more than just the momentary balance of monetary power had changed. The nation's political system was being flooded with huge, unregulated soft money contributions from corporations, labor unions and wealthy individuals.

"...RNC raised a record $16.3 million at a $1,000-a-plate gala..."

While there were only 249 members of Team 100, the list of corporations, unions and individuals who've given more than $20,000 in soft money to the political parties since January 1991 now numbers more than 1,953, and 492 of them have given at least $100,000.

This year, with both Congress and the White House up for grabs, both parties have pulled out all the stops. In January the RNC raised a record $16.3 million at a $1,000-a-plate gala, and donors who raised $250,000 or more were promised meals and meetings with top House and Senate leaders, breakfast with the party's presidential nominee and VIP seating at the GOP convention.

GOP donors are grouped according to contribution size, and various groups are accorded different privileges and meetings, says the RNC's Crawford. Donors of $100,000 and more are still considered Team 100 members, while contributors of $15,000 are designated Eagles; $5,000 donors are admitted to the Chairman's Advisory Board; and $1,000 donors are considered members of the President's Council, she says.

In preparation for their own gala affair in May—which raised $12 million—the Democrats also offered different levels of benefits for donors and fundraisers, despite President Clinton's statements against the practice. The DNC's "levels of participation" for the event ranged from $25,000 contributors ("national gala patrons") to "national gala deputy chairs," persons who contributed at least $50,000 or raised at least $100,000. They received invitations to a pre-gala dinner, a gala reception, preferred seating at the event and four tickets to a party leadership conference.

But the DNC's Amy Weiss Tobe insists the Democratic Party is not selling influence. "In the past there has been some access [for soft money donors], but not anymore," she says. "You no longer are promised dinner with the president. Our soft money donors don't have any more access than anybody else."

Meanwhile, bipartisan campaign finance reform legislation is pending in both the House and Senate. One of its provisions would put an end to the soft money system.

Fueled by Money

"There's very little difference" between the parties in their approach to soft money, conservative political analyst Kevin Phillips says with undisguised disgust. "It's one of the reasons why the Clinton administration has so little courage on so many fronts," he adds. "The parties are so thickly intertwined with this stuff, the only thing they agree on...is getting money."

Others defend the soft money system, saying the parties are only trying to keep up with the increasing amount of unregulated political spending by labor unions and issue-oriented groups like the Christian Coalition, the National Rifle Association and pro-life and pro-choice groups. "What we see in the parties is just the tip of the iceberg," says Steven Stockmeyer, executive vice president of the National Association of Business PACs and a former executive director of the National Republican Congressional Committee.

"The political parties are struggling to keep their role in a system that makes it easier for these non-party groups to spend money than the political parties," says former FEC commissioner Trevor Potter, adding that political spending by the advocacy groups isn't subject to the federal limits and disclosure rules the parties must follow. "The parties are competing in an idea marketplace with these groups that are not parties and don't have these restrictions," he says.

Stockmeyer says his group's members, who make millions of dollars in PAC contributions every year, "think the use of soft money is very healthy and don't want it to be harmed." Soft money is needed to compete with groups like the AFL-CIO, he says.

In March, RNC Chair Haley Barbour seemed to be using the labor campaign to justify more GOP spending. "We as a party are going to make an effort to offset this sort of unbelievable spending," he said, "and it will fall to us to keep the message in front of the people between now and August." However, Republican Party officials had already announced a plan to do just that—to make up for the fact that the campaign of Bob Dole had almost reached the pre-convention spending limit imposed on presidential candidates who accept public campaign funds.

There is, however, at least one important difference between the parties and labor and issue groups when it comes to the raising and spending of soft money: The political parties, unlike the other groups, have elected officials in Congress and the White House—as well as Cabinet secretaries and thousands of administration officials—who pass laws, regulate industries and control access to other powerful decision-makers. In other words, they are in a position to offer benefits for contributions.

Potter notes the almost century-long efforts to keep corporate and labor money out of politics and says the soft money system is nothing if not ironic. "People have forgotten what Watergate was all about," he says, adding, "it was the result of a particular money system."

Considering the flourishing soft money system of today, Potter says, "Maybe we're condemned to repeat the past in 25-year cycles."

Professor Corrado believes that the parties' common financial base is "one of the reasons why we see an increasing share of the electorate searching for new alternatives, wanting more options. More and more individuals are feeling like they're not represented," he says.

Houston trial lawyer and Democratic soft money giver Michael Caddell takes a more pragmatic view. "The reality," he says, "is that we have a wide-open political system that is fueled by money. And until the politicians in Washington change that system, money is important. If you want politicians and political parties who are consistent with your viewpoint to be successful you have to support them....

"If you need any further illustration," he continues, "go to a fundraiser where the president is a participant.... Whoever that person is, arguably the most powerful person in the world, will be standing in a receiving line shaking hands for three hours. Is that a good use of that man's time? Those are the kinds of questions people ought to be asking."

Corporate Gifts Help Gain Access to U.S. Governors[2]

In the past several years, a select group of the nation's biggest corporations have given millions of dollars to the National Governors' Association and an affiliated research arm. In return for their tax-deductible contributions, the corporations' lobbyists have gained unusual access to the governors' policy-making apparatus.

They take part in the governors' plenary meetings, attend receptions with governors, get briefings from the group's leaders and staff, are offered private work spaces and meeting areas at its annual gatherings and attend other events to help them "become better acquainted with governors' staffs and to share common interests," an association fact sheet says.

They also frequently attend staff meetings that develop many of the governors' policy recommendations, giving them a chance to influence the formulation of state and Federal regulations that can mean billions of dollars to participating companies.

Among them are corporations as diverse as AT&T, Exxon, General Motors, Dow Chemical, Pfizer, Blue Cross/Blue Shield, Philip Morris and Goldman, Sachs & Company.

The bipartisan governors' group defends the practice as perfectly legal and aimed only at getting the best advice on important issues. But critics say it gives the corporations a lobbying advantage unavailable to their adversaries on major policy issues.

The corporate "fellows" were actively recruited by the governors' group. Membership was restricted to no more than 100 big companies. Other interest groups, like labor unions and policy advocacy organizations, were not invited.

The results were vividly illustrated at a meeting of the governors' natural resources committee on April 16, when the corporate fellows joined in a daylong discussion on issues including electricity policy, environmental regulation by the Federal Government and pending legislation on the cleanup of toxic waste dumps.

In the afternoon, the committee asked Gregory F. Wetstone, legislative director for the Natural Resources Defense Council, a leading environmentalist group, to join a panel discussing the Clean Air Act.

Mr. Wetstone, who said he had not been invited to attend the full day's program, said later that he was surprised to find himself facing not just the state environmental officials he had

---

[2] Article by John H. Cushman Jr., from the *New York Times*, My 17 '97.

expected but also officials from big corporations that have been lobbying hard against tighter air quality standards proposed by the environmental agency. "It is very troubling that corporations are able to buy a much greater level of access than the public in general or the public-interest community," Mr. Wetstone said in an interview later.

The corporate donations—about $786,000 in 1996, the association's records show—support an entity known as the Center for Best Practices. Founded in 1974 as part of the governors' organization, it was renamed last year and is a legally distinct nonprofit corporation, but is still run by a board of four governors. The center also receives financing from philanthropic foundations and from the Federal Government.

"...in 1988, for an annual payment of up to $12,000, a company can designate one or more 'corporate fellows'..."

Under a program set up in 1988, for an annual payment of up to $12,000, a company can designate one or more "corporate fellows" who work on the center's research into social and economic policies.

As a side benefit, the participants, who are most often senior lobbyists for the corporations, rub shoulders with governors and their staffs in a way that few others can match.

The governors' group describes the program as "an unparalleled opportunity to serve as catalysts to change."

Ann McBride, the president of Common Cause, the public affairs lobby, called the arrangement "just another permutation in the way that access is being purchased in the political process."

"They are so far off base that I can't tell you," responded Gov. Tommy G. Thompson of Wisconsin, chairman of the center and former chairman of the governors' association. "We are raising money for a foundation in order to allow the Center for Best Practices, which is currently held hostage by just Federal dollars, to do more things to help the environment, help the economy, help the governors do their job better."

The organization has played an increasingly influential role in shaping Federal policy, especially by urging that Federal social and regulatory programs be delegated to state governments.

Gov. Bob Miller of Nevada, the association's chairman, said the group was beyond being swayed by special interests because it usually operated by consensus among 50 governors.

But the corporate fellows do frequently attend meetings of specialized committees of the association that recommend policies on issues of intense interest to big business, like environmental rules, tax policy and health insurance.

Association officials insisted that every meeting attended by corporate fellows was open to anybody else who wanted to attend. But because the meetings are not publicized, almost nobody but lobbyists ever attends even the open meetings.

While lobbyists for industry trade associations, Federal officials, environmentalists and other interested parties are sometimes invited to present their views at such meetings, few outsiders are involved to the extent that corporate fellows are.

One example of the policy-making sessions where corporate fellows have taken part is an association committee's deliberations over a newly drafted policy about restructuring the electric utility industry, one of the biggest economic issues facing the Federal and state governments.

Among those on the governors' list of corporate fellows are William Lhota, executive vice president of the American Electric Power Company, Steven J. Kean, senior vice president for the Enron Corporation, and Roger Schwarz, director of Federal affairs at the Public Service Electric and Gas Company of New Jersey, all corporations with major financial stakes in restructuring the electric utility industry.

But Raymond C. Scheppach, executive director of the governors' organization, said the corporations mostly supported a broader, public interest in issues like job training. "There is very little work that you would argue is business oriented in any sense of the word," he said. "A lot of it is education, early childhood education. There is very little we do that has business implications."

Corporate fellows "do sit in and listen to the discussions, and at times they do in fact give presentations," he said, but their role in policy making is modest.

But the association's fact sheet describing the program to potential participants says that the program gives "a unique opportunity" to present industry's views to governors on specific issues.

"Corporate fellows are often asked to provide private sector input on current and emerging policy issues in panel discussions, meetings and written reports," it says.

"Sure, on the marketing side, we probably have made that pitch," said the director of the center, John B. Thomasian. "It is a lot less than it is cracked up to be."

But Bill Hogan, director of investigative projects at the Center for Public Integrity, a nonpartisan research group that examines political finance issues, said that this kind of participation could be very valuable to a lobbyist. "At the simplest level, you are privy to their thoughts, deliberations, et cetera," he said. "At a higher level, perhaps you can influence them, nip something in the bud, or whatever."

Corporations Adopt a Different Attitude: Show Us the Value[3]

Avon Products used to support causes that alleviated human suffering. Today, it gives only to programs that relate specifically to women, its primary customers. So March of Dimes and lung cancer associations are out; scholarships for women, and breast and ovarian cancer groups are in. "Our giving has to be in line with our vision for the business," said Marcia L. Worthing, the senior vice president for human resources.

AT&T, which no longer makes phone equipment, has stopped financing charities in foreign countries where it had manufacturing plants. It is funneling the money to Internet-related education programs in California, Illinois and the handful of other states where it has introduced local phone service. "We're investing in communities and causes that represent our primary markets," said Timothy J. McClimon, the executive director of the AT&T Foundation.

Say goodbye to the days when corporations blithely wrote checks to many worthy causes—or to all groups that counted the chairman's spouse on its board. Say hello instead to the new world of "strategic giving," the fancy phrase that corporate-giving gurus use to describe how every dollar or product they give must mesh with the company's markets or employees.

"Corporate philanthropy has always brushed up against marketing, public relations, government relations and human resource management," said Craig Smith, a senior fellow at the Conference Board in New York, which researches corporate trends. "But now companies are far more explicit about using it as a subtle means of manipulation."

Most corporate chiefs would bridle at Mr. Smith's wording, but few would disagree with his premise. "The chief executives are all asking, What kind of value are we getting for our investment?" said Curt Weeden, the vice president of corporate contributions at Johnson & Johnson. Paul M. Ostergard, the head of the Citicorp Foundation, added, "It's a lot easier to persuade top management to increase philanthropic giving when they're certain it addresses the right priorities."

In a sense, the trend is a logical extension of the strategic changes that have swept corporate America in the 90's. One by one, companies have dispensed with sentimentality and shed longtime products and services that no longer provided the best return on investment. Corning no longer makes Corningware; Monsanto has moved out of basic chemicals; Westinghouse is

---

[3] Article by Claudia H. Deutsch, from the *New York Times*, D 9 '97 p12.

exiting everything but radio and television.

Inevitably, charities have fallen prey to the same paring knife. The Metropolitan Opera or the American Cancer Society or the local Little League club might have been on the giving list for decades. But if the cause does not somehow support the core business, it is out.

Companies have not used strategic giving as a flimsy excuse to get stingy, though. According to the Conference Board, American companies and their foundations donated $8.5 billion in cash and products last year, up from $7.9 billion in 1995. Although a growing number of those dollars are leaving the country as companies try to shore up their images overseas, that still leaves ample sums for American causes.

Chief executives are also proving to have deep pockets. Bill Gates, for example, has earmarked $200 million of his personal money to connect libraries to the Internet. And Ted Turner, the founder of CNN and Time Warner's vice-chairman, has pledged a total of $1 billion to the United Nations.

"Bill Gates... has earmarked $200 million of his personal money to connect libraries to the Internet."

A growing number of companies match any employee's charitable donation, whether or not the charity is on the strategic list. Many companies also offer grants to causes at which employees—or, better still, teams of employees—volunteer.

Take the American Express Foundation. It will give away $23.2 million this year, mostly to historic preservation, arts and education programs that tie in with its financial services or travel and tourism businesses. Yet over the last three years, it has given almost $850,000 to diverse causes that include an organic garden project, a traveling mammography van and a cat rescue program. The unifying theme: American Express employees work as volunteers with the groups sponsoring those programs, and the company sees the program as yet another employee benefit.

"We can't give to everything that comes over the transom," said Mary Beth Salerno, the foundation's president, "but we do want to give to causes that are important to our employees."

But few corporations are as benevolent as their numbers indicate. An increasing chunk of corporate contributions are in the form of products or services, which companies can value at their retail prices but manufacture for far less. Last year's tax-law changes made the economics of that approach even more compelling: companies donating $1 in cash can write off $1; by contrast, companies donating a product that costs $1 to make but sells for $3 can write off $2—the cost plus half the difference between the cost and the fair-market value.

To further sweeten the deal, donated products act as a showcase. When Johnson & Johnson sends drugs to a disaster area, more doctors grow familiar with those products. When Avon donates cosmetics to a homeless shelter, the products—and the company's largess—are displayed to social workers, family members, doctors and others with more buying power than the immediate recipients.

"We are putting products into the community," Ms. Worthing said. Products accounted for about $6 million of Avon's $18.6 million in contributions last year, she added.

Few companies are contrite about the tilt toward products. Most insist—and many nonprofit groups agree—that the charities would have to buy the products anyway and couldn't care less about how the companies value them on their books.

"We give in ways that help the recipients the most," said Barbara Dingfield, the director of community affairs for Microsoft. Although cash accounted for only about $11.1 million of Microsoft's $73.2 million in contributions last year, Ms. Dingfield noted that the company had given scholarships to women and members of minorities who want to study computer science and given cash grants to libraries nationwide as well as to community programs in the Puget Sound region in Washington, where Microsoft has its headquarters.

"Johnson & Johnson...will give away $52 million in cash and $70 million in products this year..."

Moreover, corporations say that if they are to be castigated for overinflating the dollar value of their gifts, they should also be praised for not quantifying the countless hours of employee time they donate.

"By itself, checkbook philanthropy is going to be ineffective in getting disadvantaged kids on a college-bound track," said Mr. Ostergard of Citibank, whose employees and retirees mentor children and teach classes in schools that Citibank supports with cash.

General Electric also sends employees and retirees into schools as mentors and tutors and into community groups as team leaders and organizers. It recently committed one million employee-hours to America's Promise, a White House-sponsored program to help troubled children. And it has started a program to send administrators of nonprofit groups through classes in management techniques led by G.E. managers. The aim is to make sure nonprofits get the maximum bang for G.E.'s donated buck. (That's the carrot. The stick is that G.E. cuts off any charity that cannot show that it is putting its money to good use.)

"We are leveraging our grants and gifts of product through our people," said Jane L. Polin, the program manager of the General Electric Fund, which dispenses about $30 million a year.

Add to that "and through the press." Corporations are becoming quite adept at pushing news of their generosity into the papers and onto the airwaves.

"We get a lot of exposure for our work, and that is not accidental," said Mr. McClimon of AT&T. "We write press releases, advertise events and spend a lot of time making sure the publicity machines at the nonprofit organizations are rolling along."

If there is one overarching force driving philanthropic triage at corporations today, it is the chance for good exposure to an important constituency. American Express is helping train welfare recipients for jobs at a Pennsylvania mall. Why? "The retail industry is a very important customer of ours," Ms. Salerno said.

The giving landscape abounds with such examples. Johnson & Johnson, which will give away $52 million in cash and $70 million in products this year, will direct most of the money to hospital-related causes, like medical research and management education for nurses and administrators. But it will also give a large sum to Head Start, which helps disadvantaged youngsters prepare for elementary school.

The link? Head Start has a health-care component, and "our affiliation gives us tremendous good will with doctors and dentists and in Washington," Mr. Weeden said.

Similarly, 80 percent of the $35 million that the Citicorp Foundation will give away this year will go to community development and education programs, particularly those that give lower-income people upward mobility by providing things like loans and schooling. But Citicorp will still give sizable sums to the arts—including high-profile opera and concert companies that already have wealthy patrons. "That kind of support is pretty important to our private banking customers," Mr. Ostergard said.

Indeed, at some companies the new strategic focus has brought more, not fewer, causes under the philanthropic roof.

Bristol-Myers Squibb, a pharmaceutical and personal-care product company, had for decades directed its donations almost exclusively to medical research. Three years ago, at the behest of a new chief executive, the company's foundation broadened its concept of strategic giving. Now it also gives to women's health-education programs—a tie-in with its Clairol line of women's products as well as its drug lines—and to science education programs that might interest children in pursuing research or medical careers.

"We try to identify issues that have an impact on all our divisions," said John L. Damonti, the president of the foundation, which gave out $22 million last year. "We want people to look at our grants and understand what our company is all about."

Companies for the Cure[4]

Breast cancer has become the corporate cause of the moment. As a result, some big guns are firing powerful salvos on women's behalf.

Four years ago, at the age of 63, my mother died of breast cancer. Two of her sisters and one of her aunts also have the disease and, as of this moment, are survivors. Every day of every month of every year, I am perilously conscious of the epidemic. I know all the statistics by heart: that breast cancer is the number one cause of cancer death among women in their 40s, that 180,200 new cases will be diagnosed this year alone, and that 43,900 women will die.

Those numbers are part of what is driving the current war on breast cancer—a war being waged increasingly on the corporate front as businesses large and small embrace this disease as their cause. Everywhere are hopeful signs that companies, as much as individual women, are desperate to make a difference. Kellogg Co. provides pink "survivor" caps and buttons to women who participate in the Race for the Cure fund-raisers of the Susan G. Komen Breast Cancer Foundation. Regis Hairstylists offers $10 "Clip for the Cure" cuts one day a year at its eight hundred salons. And just last month, the first BMW-sponsored Drive for the Cure, a cross-country caravan that raised money with each mile it traveled, ended its six-month tour.

But raising money is only half the effort. Many companies contribute to the campaign to raise awareness, to keep the issue at the front of women's minds. During the first Women's National Basketball Association games in July, Lee Apparel Co., the jeans maker, distributed thousands of pink ribbons. New Balance sews pink ribbons in some of its athletic shoes. Titleist makes a pink-ribbon-imprinted golf ball.

Breast cancer's role as the high-profile cause of the '90s was assured in June, at the auction of Princess Diana's wardrobe. Half the proceeds went to the Evelyn H. Lauder Breast Center at Memorial Sloan Kettering Cancer Center in Manhattan. "It was an incredibly glamorous evening," says Lauder, who founded the center in 1993, of the pre-auction party for eight hundred given by Christie's two nights before the sale. "I looked around and realized that we had finally arrived. Breast Cancer was literally out of the closet."

It wasn't always this way. Following are a few key battles in the war, great corporate moments of the past decade that continue to make a difference.

---

[4] Article by Jan Jarboe Russell, a freelance writer in San Antonio, TX, from *Working Woman* 22/11:62-64 N '97. Copyright © 1997 by MacDonald Communications Corporation. Reprinted with permission.

Zeneca: In March 1985, the top executives of Zeneca, the manufacturer of tamoxifen, the most widely used hormone treatment for patients with breast cancer, met in New York with account executives at public relations firm Burson-Marsteller and ad agency Sudler & Hennessey to discuss how to package the breast cancer message. "It was still the early stages," recalls Zeneca's Steve Lampert. "Our goal was to find a way to warn people about the disease without scaring them to death." What was needed, they decided, was a safe face. The obvious choice was former first lady Betty Ford, who became one of the first celebrities to discuss the disease publicly when her own breast cancer was diagnosed in 1974. But Ford was 67. They needed to target a younger generation. How about Ford's daughter, Susan Ford Bales, someone suggested. "Susan was very close to her mother, and her memories of how she felt as a teenager when her mother was diagnosed were clear and fresh," Lampert says. Bales agreed to become the national spokesperson for what was then called National Breast Cancer Awareness Week—what we now know as National Breast Cancer Awareness Month, a public education campaign sponsored by seventeen cancer advocacy groups but funded entirely by Zeneca. After all these years, Bales is still the face behind the charity.

"...Betty Ford... became one of the first celebrities to discuss...her own breast cancer... diagnosed in 1974."

Revlon: Like other cancer researchers, Dennis Slamon's goal is to develop a vaccine to eradicate breast cancer. But in August 1989, the University of Southern California scientist was running out of money for his research into the genetic causes of the disease. He appealed to Ronald Perelman, chairman of Revlon. At a meeting with Perelman and one of his vice presidents, James Conroy, Slamon explained that the wait for money from the National Institutes of Health or the American Cancer Society could delay progress in his lab for as long as two years. "By the time the money comes through, another one hundred thousand women will be dead," said one of the doctors present. "That's enough to fill the entire Rose Bowl." The image was so chilling it prompted Perelman to hand over $2.5 million to help finance Slamon's research.

Since 1989, Revlon has given more than $12 million for research and sponsored such fund-raising events as the Fire and Ice Ball and an annual Los Angeles five-kilometer run. But it's the grim image of the Rose Bowl Conroy can never forget—an offhand comment that got Perelman's attention and helped change the way cancer research is funded in America. These days, corporations routinely provide stopgap funding for programs until federal money arrives.

Metrolina Outreach Mammography: In 1992, Jean Griswold quit her job as a medical-equipment sales and marketing manager, borrowed half a million dollars, and founded Metrolina Outreach Mammography in Charlotte, North Carolina. She'd been wanting to do it for seven years, ever since, as a manager at Technomed USA, she had negotiated the sale of the first mobile mammography unit in the country to the University of California at San Francisco. At that time, the cost of the equipment was so high that only hospitals and universities offered such services. "Logically, I knew it made no sense," Griswold says of her plan to go solo, "but I just couldn't let go of the idea."

Since then, she has contracted with more than a hundred employers and agencies to offer mammograms to women at workplaces in North and South Carolina, Georgia, and Virginia. She screens more than six thousand women a year, primarily the working poor who earn less than $12,000. In the last five years, she has given mammograms in factory lunchrooms, in church basements, in battered women's shelters. Griswold never turns anyone away. If she can't find an employer willing to pay, she raises money from individual donors or churches, or through Mobile Health Outreach, a not-for-profit foundation she formed to pay for mammograms for women who can't afford them. "People in big cities have the idea that every woman knows she should have a mammogram by age 40," says Griswold. "Well, that's an urban myth."

"...Y-Me...hotline had a 60 percent increase in calls, a third of which came in after 5."

Boston Market: In the fall of 1995, executives of Boston Market, an upscale fast-food chain of twelve hundred restaurants, wanted to ride the wave of breast cancer charity but knew their company was too small to fund significant research. Instead they partnered with Y-Me, a Chicago-based organization that provides a national hotline for counseling women with breast cancer and their families. At the time, says patient services director Michelle Melin, the hotline received eighteen thousand calls a year, but they were toll-free only between 9 AM and 5 PM; after that, callers had to pick up the expense. Tom Beck, a Boston Market vice president, asked a simple question: "What happens if you find a lump in your breast after 5 PM and need to talk?" That question defined the scope of Boston Market's work.

Within the next few months, the takeout chain made it possible to call toll-free twenty-four hours a day, upgraded Y-Me telephone lines, provided computers and voice mail, and designed a Web page (www.y-me.org). Cards with Y-Me's number were also placed in Boston Market stores in thirty-eight states, explaining that volunteers were on duty day and night to offer emotional support and information about treatment. Last year, the hotline had a 60 percent increase in calls, a third of which came in after 5. One of those calls was from a woman who had stopped at Boston Market to pick up dinner for her family after being told she had breast cancer. "I don't feel so alone," she said.

Bristol-Myers Squibb: Although black women are diagnosed with breast cancer in about the same proportion as the rest of the population, their mortality rate is higher, primarily because they don't discover the disease as early. "Among African-Americans, the subject is still too frightening to talk about," says Dr. Georgia Robins Sadler, a health care researcher at the University of California at San Diego. "That's the barrier we need to break."

In January 1997, Sadler thought she'd found a way to do it. She had just completed a study showing that a group of African-American beauticians in San Diego were able to provide information to their clients about breast cancer—how to perform breast self-exams, the importance of mammography and regular breast checkups—while styling their hair. "What we demonstrated is that the beauticians were absolutely the most natural people in the world to reach this population," Sadler says. "Having your hair done is a feel-good time for women, a private indulgence, and the beauticians could talk to their clients about breast cancer in a way that did not scare them to death. The women were more comfortable talking to their beauticians than to doctors."

It wasn't quite that simple, though. Beauticians would have to be trained to deliver accurate information, perhaps even provided with videotapes and other educational tools. Sadler had no money for such a program—until she got a call from Mari Claire Payawal, the director of the Bristol-Myers Squibb Foundation. Payawal had heard about Sadler's research, which sparked her interest. Bristol-Myers, one of the giants of cancer pharmaceuticals, is the maker of Taxol, the drug most often used after the initial chemotherapy. The company spends millions each year on research for new treatments. The fact that it was seeking out such a small, relatively unknown program came as a surprise.

"I sent the results of our preliminary study, asked for $300,000, and crossed my fingers," says Sadler. Within a few months, Payawal called back—the check was in the mail. Now Sadler is developing a nationwide model for beauticians in high-risk communities.

Miracle on 42nd St.[5]

Every New Yorker has a Times Square story. Rudolph Giuliani, the city's high-strung mayor, fondly recalls trips to see the comedy team of Dean Martin and Jerry Lewis at the Paramount theater. "They were my favorite comedians as a youngster," Giuliani recalls. "The crowds would spill right out onto Times Square. It would almost be like a New Year's Eve celebration. Dean and Jerry would hang out the window of their dressing room and throw programs and things down to their fans." According to Giuliani, Times Square in those days was "the center of the world"—just the sort of boosterish hyperbole one expects from a New York City mayor. But Giuliani does have a point. Times Square probably has as great a hold on the nation's imagination as any piece of American real estate: The Great White Way! Bobby-soxers and Frank Sinatra! V-E day!

Ratso Rizzo! Porn! Human scum!

Here's another Times Square story, set a few decades after Giuliani's and told by Maria Alvarado, coordinator of tourism services for the Times Square Business Improvement District: "One summer, when I was about to give birth to my first child, I came down to have lunch with my husband, who worked on 43rd and Sixth. I took the E train, so I had to walk down 42nd. Here I was, eight months pregnant, and I was offered everything from sex to cocaine. Eight months pregnant, and they wouldn't leave me alone." She is referring, of course, not to Martin and Lewis but to the pimps, hustlers and drug dealers who by the 1970s had replaced sailors as perhaps the area's most emblematic denizens.

Decline and fall is a familiar urban arc. But out-of-towners whose lurid visions of Times Square have been formed by movies like *Midnight Cowboy* and *Taxi Driver*—or shocking discoveries made after taking a wrong turn on the way from the tour bus to *Victor/Victoria*—might be surprised by the extent to which the area is approaching the millennium in a clean and sober state. That is, if "sober" fairly applies to a cityscape that has become more enthusiastically garish than ever thanks to the capabilities of modern signage. Tourism is rising; crime is dropping, at an even faster clip than in the rest of the city. The area is bustling with new hotels, new office buildings—not to mention new chain stores and corny theme restaurants that would be at home in any suburban mall. Not that Times Square (which technically refers only to the triangle above 42nd Street where Broadway and Seventh Avenue meet but casually takes in the entire neighborhood) doesn't still retain some of its seedy, pre-

[5] Article by Bruce Handy, from *Time* 149/14:68-72 Ap 7 '97. Copyright © 1997 Time, Inc. Reprinted with permission.

Gap allure. Indeed, sailors still flock here during Fleet Week, but last year they were reportedly heard complaining that prostitutes had grown scarce.

This week the public will get its first look at the most spectacular fruit yet of the area's renaissance: the unveiling of the Walt Disney Co.'s $34 million restoration of the New Amsterdam theater. Originally built in 1903 and famously taken over by Florenz Ziegfeld 10 years later, it is, after its refurbishment, one of the grandest and most mind-bendingly ornate theaters in America, an eclectic mélange of Art Nouveau and other turn-of-the-century ornamentation and a triumph of the restorer's art. Disney is hoping the New Amsterdam will be an economic triumph too, as home to a lucrative stream of wildly successful Disney stage shows. First up, in May, is a concert version of *King David*, a new musical by Alan Menken and Tim Rice.

The New Amsterdam—and more to the point. Disney's corporate presence and the vote of confidence it represents—is the anchor for an ambitious city and state plan to make over 42nd Street, long the area's most notorious thoroughfare. As the sleaziest strip in the sleaziest part of town, the stretch of 42nd Street between Seventh and Eighth avenues was from the late '60s until just a few years ago the ninth circle of Times Square. "You could buy anything you wanted, whether it was drugs or girls or boys or green cards or telephone cards. You really felt like you were walking through this hellish zone," says Cora Cahan, president of the New 42nd Street Inc., which is overseeing the restoration of seven of the strip's nine theaters. Back in 1978 more than twice as many street crimes were reported on the block as on any other block in the entire city. In 1984 the city-planning-commission chairman told *New York* magazine that 42nd "is the one street where the city has lost control."

"Back in 1978 more than twice as many street crimes were reported on... [42nd Street] as on any other block in the entire city."

Today the block is well on its way to becoming Manhattan's most chipper. On its east end a onetime porno palace—where Robert De Niro took Cybill Shepherd on an ill-fated date in *Taxi Driver*—is now a children's theater. Across the street, next to the New Amsterdam, is a big, bright Disney store—probably the only Disney store in the world that is just four doors away from an establishment that sells scary-looking swords and knives, boxing equipment and dusty copies of Bruce Lee videos. The latter retailer is one of two storefront businesses that remain from the street's previous incarnation. The other is a narrow little wedge of lunch counter; yellowed signs that read NO LOITERING and PLEASE PAY WHEN SERVED linger as warnings to a pre-urban renewal clientele.

The rest of the old establishments, largely porn emporiums and small shops selling cheap consumer goods, have been evicted. Gone too is the sick-sweet odor of mildew and disinfectant that used to permeate the block, a calling card for its unwholesome diversions. If all goes according to plan, their place will be taken by, among many other things, the Ford Center for the Performing

Arts (a new megatheater for musicals combining two of the street's original stages), vast multiplex movie theaters and more tourist lures like Madame Tussaud's Wax Museum.

Once the home of John Barrymore, Eddie Cantor and Fanny Brice, 42nd Street began to decline with the Crash of 1929, which bankrupted a number of the theater owners, turning legitimate stages into burlesque houses and movie theaters. Even in Giuliani's youth questionable entertainments were a staple (the future mayor could have paid to see a man eat live mice at Hubert's Museum and Flea Circus). The postwar exodus of the city's middle class continued the block's slow skid into porndom.

It's a neat irony, then, that the crash of 1987 is in great part responsible for 42nd Street's rebirth as a middle-class destination. Earlier in the decade the city and state agreed on an ambitious $2.5 billion redevelopment plan for 42nd Street and Times Square, the driving force of which was to be four mammoth, nearly identical office towers designed by Philip Johnson and John Burgee as a kind of chilly Rockefeller Center South. Fortunately for fans of Times Square's higgledy-piggledy aesthetic, the late-'80s economic downturn pulled the rug out from under that plan. And there was this added benefit: the developers were obligated to cough up $241 million to the city and state whether or not they ever built. That kitty allowed planners to start condemning properties and evicting what they saw as undesirable tenants. Developers still have the right to erect their office towers—ground has already been broken on a building that will house the Condé Nast magazine empire—but the Johnson-Burgee designs have been chucked.

By 1993 most of the old theaters and porn shops were boarded up. Despite a building boom in the rest of the Times Square area, 42nd Street's caretakers were having a hard time interesting new tenants because a figurative stench still lingered. Of the few serious inquiries about the old theaters, one came from a mud-wrestling entrepreneur, another from Michael Eisner. Disney's chairman became interested in owning a theater in New York because the company's theatrical version of *Beauty and the Beast* was imminent on Broadway. As it happens, the architect Robert A.M. Stern, who had devised post-Johnson-Burgee guidelines for 42nd Street, is a member of Disney's board. Stern told Eisner about the New Amsterdam. On a grim winter day, Stern and Cora Cahan took Eisner, his wife and son on a tour of the theater, shuttered since 1983.

The group stumbled into a magnificent wreck. Water poured through a hole in the roof, mushrooms grew on the floor. "The theater was almost impassable," Stern recalls. "Plaster was all over the stairs, like an alpine slag heap. We each carried giant flashlights and wore hard hats. Birds were flying through, dropping their stuff as we passed. It was a mess, but of course a very romantic mess. Michael was quick to see not only the romance but the potential." What Eisner also came to see, after two years of tough negotiations, was a deal that included low-interest loans from the city and state to cover 75% of the restoration—a good deal for both sides, since Disney's involvement proved to be 42nd Street's turning point, encouraging other corporations to sign up.

Today water no longer pours through the New Amsterdam's ceiling dome, once again surrounded by a thick garland of red berries and hydrangea wreaths, blue-glazed peacocks and 10-ft.-long angels. The work involved many subtle calibrations. The architect, Hugh Hardy, aimed for a final product that would return the theater to its original state yet allow it to look as if it had been gently lived in for 30 years or so. "There is," he observes, "an inherent conflict in preservation between conservation, which means you keep everything that's original and try not to have it deteriorate further, and restoration, which is the other extreme. If you restore everything and make it look brand-new, you rob the place of a sense of history. You have to be careful not to get stuck at either extreme. It's all about memory, and memory is not science."

He's referring to the theater, but he could just as easily be talking about the block as a whole—which begs the question of whose memories you take as your signpost. Rudolph Giuliani's? Those of the kids who used to watch kung-fu movies in the old New Amsterdam? John Barrymore's? With the mix of live and canned entertainment, shopping, restaurants and tourist attractions, and with the hoped-for blend of high, middle and low brow, 42nd Street's caretakers are aiming to re-create the traditional ambiance and uses of 42nd Street in a late-'90s context. Since 42nd Street's traditional ambiance is chaotic, the city and state are in the odd position of planning something that is supposed to appear unplanned. Conundrum or not, they so far seem to have succeeded, despite critics' fears that the block would become an 800-ft.-long Disney World. "This is 42nd Street," Cahan reminds us. "It rains. Big trucks go across it. There is no climate control here. It smells. This is not City Walk at Universal City. This is a very real street. It is going to be more of what it once was than ever."

One hopes that will include at least a little room for organic, noncorporate funk. "I would like them to leave a little of New York for the old-timers, for New Yorkers," says Fred Hakim, who owns the aforementioned lunch counter and has been working in the area for 56 years. He is still waiting to find out if he will be able to continue operating in his space.

IV. The Corporation and the Media

Editor's Introduction

The final section of this compilation discusses corporate ownership of the media. Recent corporate acquisition of broadcast and print information sources, be they news-oriented or not, has evoked a variety of reactions. In general, many worry that as newspapers, publishing houses, and television and cable stations come under common corporate ownership, the freedom to decide what should be published or reported will be subjugated to a corporate agenda. For example, what happens when a television station wants to report a story that reveals information that is not in the interest of the corporate-owner? Will bottom-line profit and loss concerns become the sole criterion in deciding what is published and what is not? Or, will corporate executives leave journalists alone and let them continue reporting as they did prior to corporate ownership?

This section begins with an article containing a chart, reprinted from *The Nation* magazine, outlining corporate ownership (as of June 1996) of magazines, publishing houses, and television and cable stations. As the chart reveals, the bulk of the mass media is owned by a few corporations. Following the chart, various broadcast and print media leaders provide their insights into the issue. Acclaimed television producer Norman Lear is careful to note that "there are no villains" in this situation, as the corporations are but "those who have succeeded in the free-enterprise system" that we espouse. Danny Schechter, on the other hand, questions the extent to which the corporation will place its own interests above the public interest when setting corporate mandates on subsidiary news organizations.

In November of 1996 the *Columbia Journalism Review* gathered a group of 250 media executives and journalists to discuss the consequences of media conglomeration, being collective ownership under a single corporation. From this article, it is evident that an exciting forum filled with differing opinions developed. Moderator Ken Auletta pointed out that "journalists are meant to prize their independence, not teamwork." The independence of the journalist could in fact be threatened in the seemingly "borderless company" that Auletta believes typifies the average corporation. Dorothy Rabinowitz pointed out that media conglomeration or not, "the enemy of the journalist has always been the herd mentality." Rabinowitz believes that it isn't "the threat of conglomerates" that causes journalists to feign the public interest, but rather "the overused term—political correctness." Rabinowitz doesn't think corporate ownership of the media will cause any dramatic changes and says that we should shift our attention to other, far more threatening issues.

A review of the documentary "Fear and Favor in the Newsroom" asserts that corporate ownership of the media amounts to little more than outright censorship. To illustrate his point, the author, Fr. Raymond A. Schroth, includes a series of case studies in which news stories that might "offend local and national corporations, which share directorships with the corporate owners of the media" have been prevented from reaching the public's ear and eye.

André Schiffrin, owner of the not-for-profit publisher The New Press, discusses the impact of corporate ownership on the publishing house. While corporations are not entirely responsible, the typical publishing house now focuses on the potential profitability of a book rather than the book's quality. According to Schiffrin, when a publisher is deciding whether to publish a book, "The question is which books will make the most money, not which ones will fulfill the publisher's traditional cultural mission." This is a consequence of several factors, the first a reduction in library budgets and the second the "new profit targets" demanded by the publishing house's controlling conglomerate. Where publishing houses used to make "around 4 percent after taxes," corporations now expect profits "in the range of 12 to 15 percent."

On That Chart[1]

We asked people in the media, academic and public interest worlds to comment on the issues raised by the outline of media ownership on pp.122–125. Their responses follow.

—The Editors

The problem with the media structure so wonderfully portrayed by your chart is not the identity of the ultimate owners—Westinghouse, Disney, GE and so on. The more basic concern is the conversion of the news business to just another corporate operation, where whoever is in charge must be as driven by the demands of the financial market as their counterparts in the banking and steel-making and fast-food industries.

Journalism has always been a business, but until now it has been sheltered from the relentless earnings pressure that affects big, publicly traded corporations. Until the past decade or so we had not experienced the news as a mainly corporate undertaking. Family owners wanted to make money, but they did not need to make the "prevailing market return" on this quarter. They did not need to worry that financial analysts would mark them down, or that mutual fund managers would start unloading their stock, if their immediate earnings fell below the industry average—or below what was available from investments anywhere else in the financial universe, from a shirt factory in Thailand to the latest Internet start-up. Now they have exactly such worries—and must respond as the new, corporatized *Los Angeles Times* did when closing *New York Newsday*. The paper was still capable of making money. It just couldn't make *enough*.

Theoretically, it is possible that this bracing market pressure will bring us some improved version of the news, as international competition spurred Detroit to bring us better cars. *The New York Times*, for instance, has responded to pressure in its home market by developing a nationwide niche audience, so that people who want a first-rate daily paper can now find one in most parts of the country. Fund managers might decide (we're back in the realm of theory now) that the way to make the most money in journalism is to invest heavily in the most interesting, compelling, valuable version of the news, which readers and viewers could not afford to be without. But the real-world evidence about corporate journalism points the other way. Within the time horizon of the typical fund manager, the way to raise earnings is to cut unnecessary costs and to concentrate the remaining money on star performers who might temporarily hold the audience.

---

[1] From *The Nation* Je 3, '96 15-28.

Peggy Charren
Founder, Action for Children's Television.

Democracy depends in part on the right to speak and to be heard. The media map depicts the dawn of a new world where three or five or ten C.E.O.s could determine who says what to whom in America. In the small sphere I am trying to influence, the merging of broadcasting, producing and animating companies is making it difficult for independent producers of children's shows to participate in the programming mix.

Just as we had to invent PBS to give the public more choices in broadcast television, so today we have to guarantee a "Public Telecommunications Map" to give voice to speech we need to hear and to insure an informed electorate. This means setting aside government dollars for the electronic soapbox, for classroom access to technology, for regional and local versions of C-Span and for programs that seek to educate.

"Media concentration will lead to more blending of editorial and commercial content..."

Media concentration will lead to more blending of editorial and commercial content, and to increasing corporate control of political debate. In short, if *The Nation* appeared on this map, there is a good chance the map would not appear in *The Nation*.

Danny Schechter
Executive producer, Globalvision; author of the forthcoming The More You Watch, the Less You Know.

Miller and Biden's useful chart does define a structural problem—a web that the federal trustbusters, if they existed, would have to confront. They diagram mounting media concentration and illustrate how mainstream media institutions gobble and are gobbled up by interests that have little use for the public interest. It is no wonder that the last thing you see in the media is who owns it, or how that ownership limits information, chokes substantive debate and narrows real programming choices.

Mickey Mouse and Westinghouse are just beginning to consolidate their control over ABC and CBS respectively. So far the networks are happy with new cash infusions. ABC is planning to launch its own twenty-four-hour CNN-style operation, while the CBS network is thankful to be rid of Larry Tisch, who in the pre-merger days strip-mined it. The threat there so far—this is not on the chart—is what is happening to the affiliates. At KMOX in St. Louis, for example, Westinghouse demanded that the local CBS radio affiliate double its profit performance by the next quarter, from 22 percent to nearly 50 percent. Unfortunately, raising profits means losing jobs. Ten went down the downsizer Kevin Horrigan, co-host of the station's *Morning Meeting*, remarked: "There's really no pride in working for a 'property.' It used to be a special place to work. It's not anymore. KMOX will be KDKA will be WCCO will be KCBS. These are like McDonald's restaurants."

Issues like this are off these charts. And so is PBS, which has marched steadily rightward. Its takeover has been internal, prodded by pressure from Congress and a timid leadership concerned about preserving sinecures. After four years, the human rights series I co-produce with Charlayne Hunter-Gault, Globalvision's *Rights & Wrongs*, still appears on only half the PBS stations—up quite a few since last season—and is not distributed by the PBS national bureaucracy. One of our funders, the Independent Television Service (I.T.V.S.), is being threatened with defunding with the complicity of the Corporation for Public Broadcasting. Democratizing public media is as critical as criticizing corporate media.

So what we need to map now is where we go from here. The Media & Democracy Congress generated some ideas and so did the new Cultural Environment Movement. You don't need a mapmaker to know that we need to build a movement to put media reform on the agenda—before we are all off the charts.

Norman Lear
Producer, All in the Family, Maude *and many other shows.*

Miller and Biden's map of media concentration is like the picture that speaks a thousand (in this case a million) words. It should be clear to any reasonable person that there are too few funnels through which will flow most of the world's entertainment and information. Too few funnels suggests too few individuals making too many decisions about what the world's population needs to know. It's important to remember that there are no villians here. The individuals who wield this unprecedented power have succeeded in the free-enterprise system; they are winners the culture esteems and most of us wish to become.

Herbert I. Schiller
Author, Information Inequality: The Deepening Social Crisis in America.

The United States' global industrial pre-eminence may be slipping, but the domestic output and international sale of one of its manufactures is booming—packaged consciousness. Packaged consciousness—a one-dimensional, smooth-edged cultural product—is made by the ever-expanding goliaths of the message and image business. Gigantic entertainment-information complexes exercise a near-seamless and unified private corporate control over what we think, and think about. The national symbolic environment has been appropriated by a few corporate juggernauts in the consciousness business.

No matter how many editors, producers, filmmakers, artists, photographers, musicians et al. labor in cultural factories with what we, and they, are assured is autonomy, in the end they are all subject to the overriding corporate imperative—make a profit, indeed, a steadily increasing profit.

With this holy commandment in place, the inevitable outcome

THE NATIONAL ENTERTAINMENT STATE

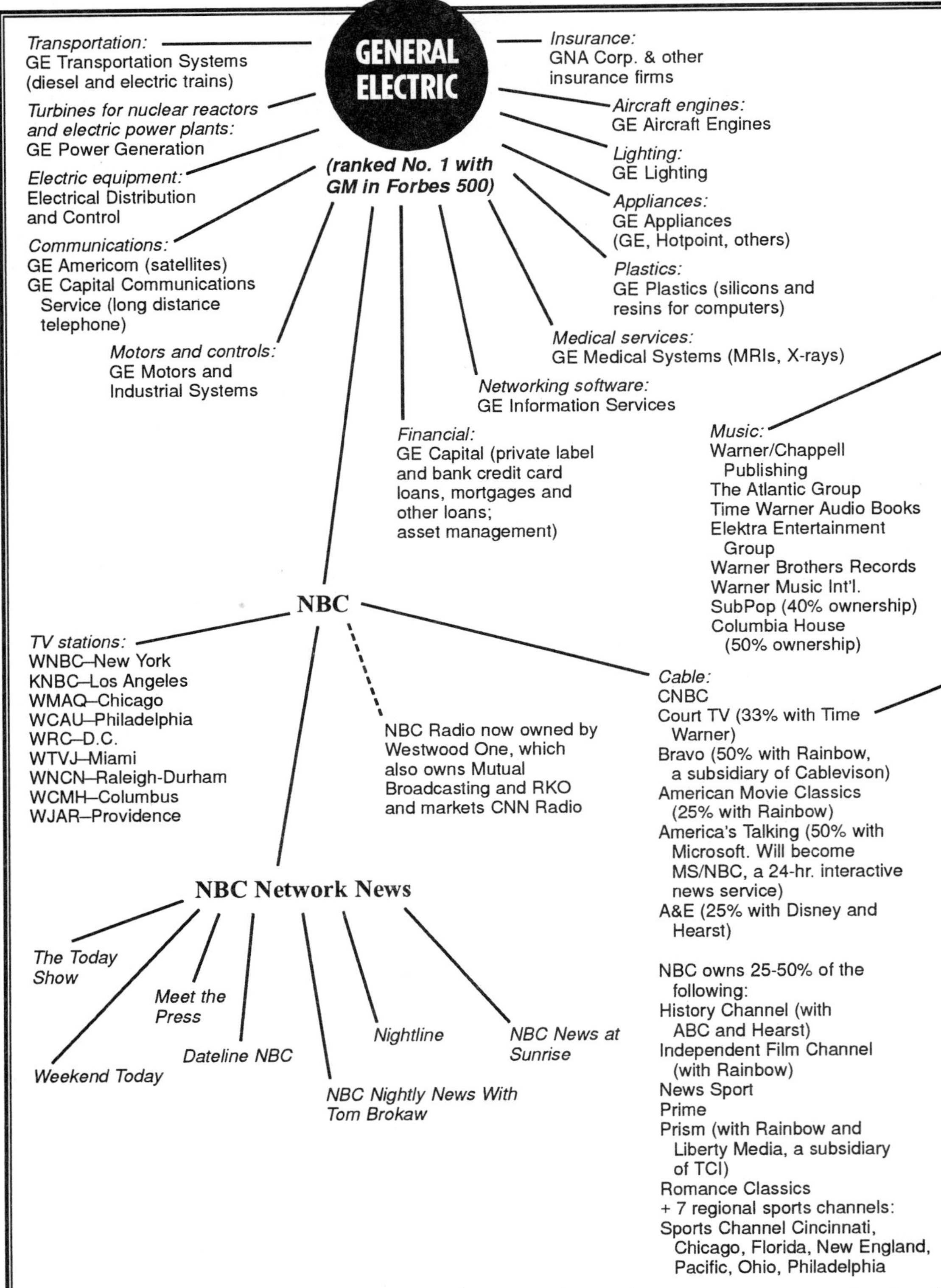

THE NATIONAL ENTERTAINMENT STATE

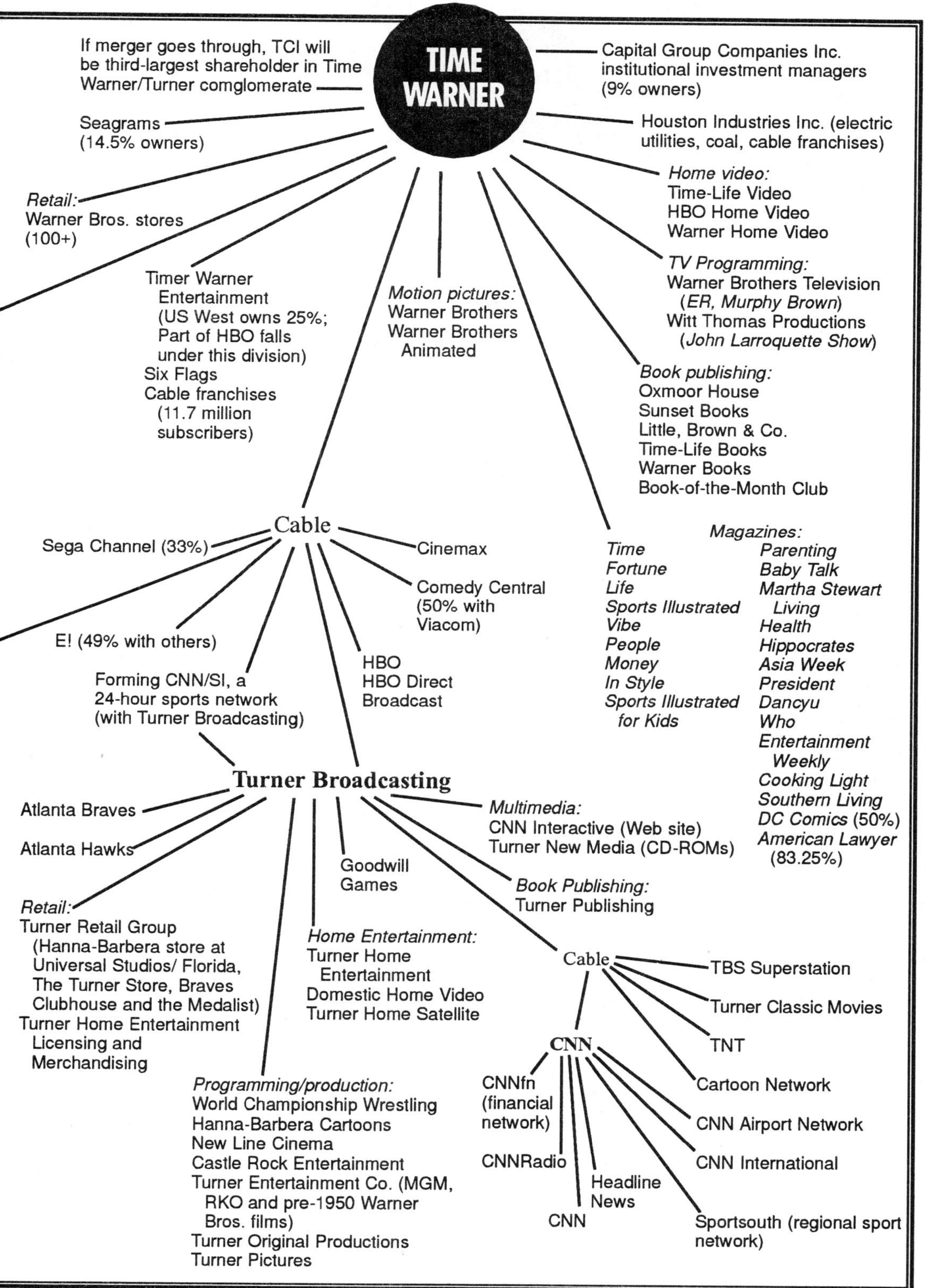

THE NATIONAL ENTERTAINMENT STATE

DISNEY/ CAP CITIES

(ranked No.48 in Forbes 500)

Sid R. Bass et al. (crude petroleum and natural gas production, 6.02% owners before merger)*

Berkshire Hathaway Inc. (Insurance; Warren Buffet, C.E.O.; ranked No. 60 in Forbes 500; 12% owners prior to merger with Disney)*

State Farm Insurance (6% owners prior to merger)*

Multimedia:
Disney Interactive
Disney.com
Americast (with some Baby Bell companies; in development)
ABC Online (interactive network for America Online)

Home video:
Buena Vista

Book publishing:
Hyperion Books
Chilton Publications

Motion pictures:
Walt Disney Pictures
Touchstone Pictures
Hollywood Pictures
Miramax Film Corp.
Buena Vista Pictures (distribution arm)

Magazines:
Chilton Publications (trade publications)
Fairchild Publications (*W., Women's Wear Daily*)
L.A. Magazine
Institutional Investor
Disney Publishing Inc. (*FamilyFun* and others)

Retail:
429 Disney stores
Childcraft Education (mail order toys)

TV and cable:
Disney Channel
Disney Television(58 hours/ week syndicated programming)
Touchstone Television (*Ellen, Home Improvement*)
A&E (37% with Hearst and GE)
Lifetime Network (50%)
ESPN (80%)
ESPN 2 (80%)
Buena Vista Television (*Home Again*)

Music:
Hollywood Records
Wonderland Music
Walt Disney Records

Mighty Ducks (N.H. L. ice hockey team)
California Angels (American League baseball team; 25% ownership and controlling interest, with option to buy remaining shares upon the death of Gene Autry)

Newspapers:
Fort Worth Star-Telegram
Kansas City Star
St. Louis Daily Record
Narragansett Times
Oakland Press and Reminder (Pontiac, MI)
County Press (Lapeer, MI)
Times-Leader (Wilkes-Barre, PA)
Belleville News-Democrat (IL)
Albany Democrat (OR)
Daily Tidings (Ashland, OR)
Sutton Industries and *Penny Power* (shoppers)

ABC

ABC Radio (owns 21 stations, largest radio network in U.S., serving 3,400 stations and covering 24% of U.S. households)

ABC Video

TV stations (covering 24.5% of US. households):
WABC–New York
WLS–Chicago
KFSN–Fresno
KTRK–Houston
WPVI–Philadelphia
KGO–San Francisco
WTVD–Raleigh-Durham
WJRT–Flint, MI
WTVG–Toledo
KABC–Los Angeles
(KCAL in L.A. for sale by agreement with Justice Dept.)

Also owns 14% interest in Young Broadcasting, which owns:
WTVO–Rockford, IL
WTEN–Albany, NY
WLNS–Lansing, MI
KLFY–Lafayette, LA
WKRN–Nashville, TN
WATE–Knoxville, TN
WRIC–Richmond, VA
WBAY–Green Bay, WI

ABC Network News

Prime Time Live
Good Morning America
Good Morning America (Sunday)
World News This Morning
World News Tonight (Saturday and Sunday editions)
World News Tonight With Peter Jennings
This Week With David Brinkley
World News Now
Nightline
20/20

*Ownership percentages are not finalized. Because 82% of stockholders opted for shares and not cash, Disney is still working out with shareholders whether they will be paid in fractional shares or with partial cash payments.

THE NATIONAL ENTERTAINMENT STATE

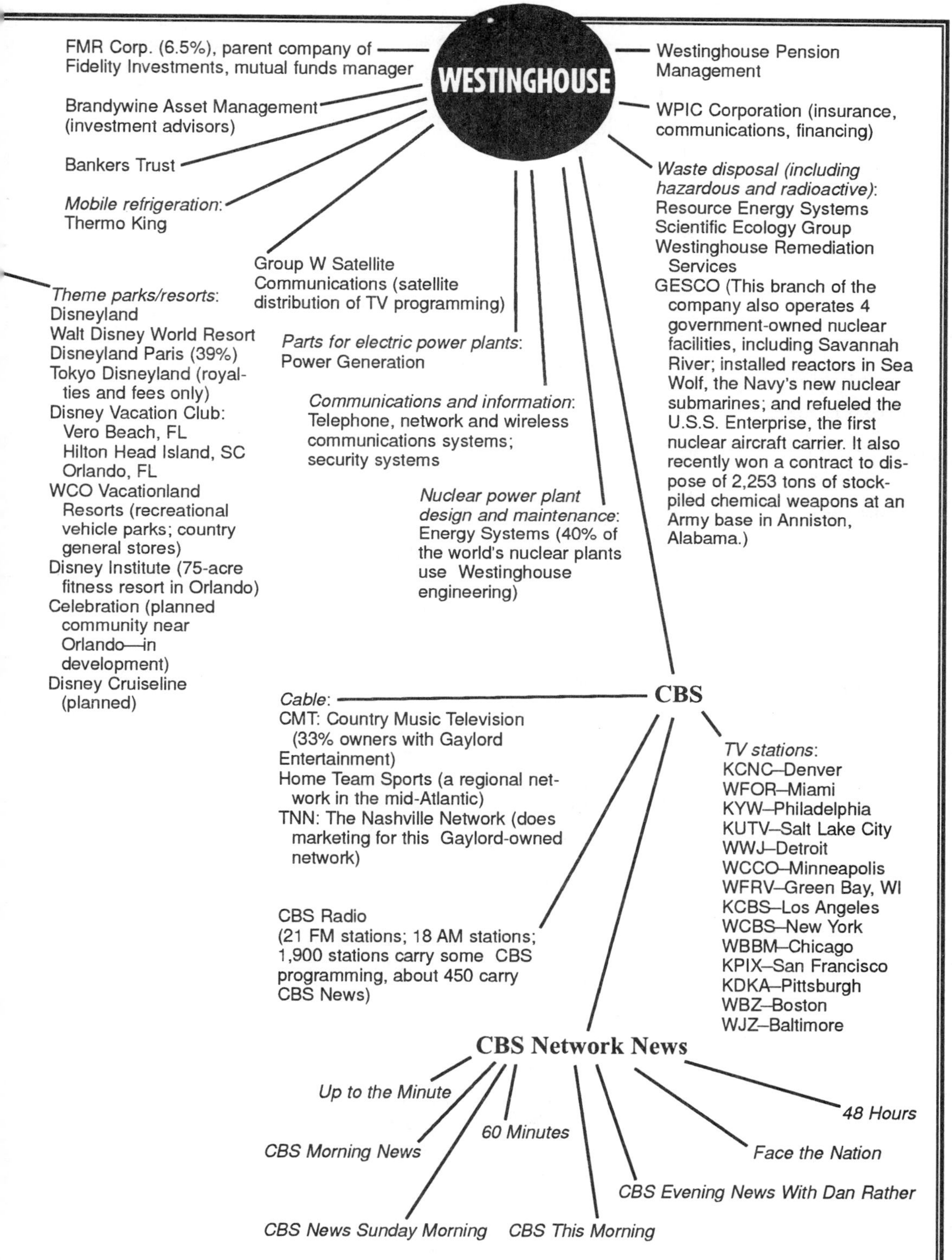

WESTINGHOUSE

FMR Corp. (6.5%), parent company of Fidelity Investments, mutual funds manager

Brandywine Asset Management (investment advisors)

Bankers Trust

Mobile refrigeration: Thermo King

Group W Satellite Communications (satellite distribution of TV programming)

Parts for electric power plants: Power Generation

Communications and information: Telephone, network and wireless communications systems; security systems

Nuclear power plant design and maintenance: Energy Systems (40% of the world's nuclear plants use Westinghouse engineering)

Westinghouse Pension Management

WPIC Corporation (insurance, communications, financing)

Waste disposal (including hazardous and radioactive):
Resource Energy Systems
Scientific Ecology Group
Westinghouse Remediation Services
GESCO (This branch of the company also operates 4 government-owned nuclear facilities, including Savannah River; installed reactors in Sea Wolf, the Navy's new nuclear submarines; and refueled the U.S.S. Enterprise, the first nuclear aircraft carrier. It also recently won a contract to dispose of 2,253 tons of stockpiled chemical weapons at an Army base in Anniston, Alabama.)

Theme parks/resorts:
Disneyland
Walt Disney World Resort
Disneyland Paris (39%)
Tokyo Disneyland (royalties and fees only)
Disney Vacation Club:
Vero Beach, FL
Hilton Head Island, SC
Orlando, FL
WCO Vacationland Resorts (recreational vehicle parks; country general stores)
Disney Institute (75-acre fitness resort in Orlando)
Celebration (planned community near Orlando—in development)
Disney Cruiseline (planned)

CBS

Cable:
CMT: Country Music Television (33% owners with Gaylord Entertainment)
Home Team Sports (a regional network in the mid-Atlantic)
TNN: The Nashville Network (does marketing for this Gaylord-owned network)

CBS Radio
(21 FM stations; 18 AM stations; 1,900 stations carry some CBS programming, about 450 carry CBS News)

TV stations:
KCNC–Denver
WFOR–Miami
KYW–Philadelphia
KUTV–Salt Lake City
WWJ–Detroit
WCCO–Minneapolis
WFRV–Green Bay, WI
KCBS–Los Angeles
WCBS–New York
WBBM–Chicago
KPIX–San Francisco
KDKA–Pittsburgh
WBZ–Boston
WJZ–Baltimore

CBS Network News

Up to the Minute
CBS Morning News
60 Minutes
CBS News Sunday Morning
CBS This Morning
CBS Evening News With Dan Rather
Face the Nation
48 Hours

[Chart reflects coporate ownership as of June 1996]

is a cultural product that is short on bite and long on safe formulas for crowd control. The "news," for instance, doesn't have to be but invariably is a nightly extravaganza of mayhem, fires, train wrecks, highway disasters and personal tragedies.

What is needed is the opening up of the image-producing structures to genuine diversity. There is a wealth of creativity in the country. Time Warner, Disney-ABC, GE-NBC, etc. should not be the exclusive channelers of it for their barren balance-sheet ends. Only political action can bring about the vast expansion that is required. The nation's concerned parents, anxious consumers, coerced workers and cohorts of dissatisfied media-entertainment-information workers must first coalesce around the urgent need to recognize that what goes into our heads and minds is of at least as much importance as what goes into our stomachs.

"Reporters and editorial boards decide what is 'the story' of the day..."

Oliver Stone

Director, Nixon, JFK, Platoon *and other movies.*

What is the difference between *Time* and *Newsweek*? Between ABC, NBC and CBS News? Between *The Washington Post* and *The New York Times*? For all practical purposes, none. The concentration of media power means that Americans increasingly get their information from a few sources who decide what is "news."

The pack mentality of the press contributes to this phenomenon. Reporters and editorial boards decide what is "the story" of the day, and they all pursue it in a feeding frenzy. Meanwhile, real investigative journalism is neglected.

To some extent, the Internet provides a solution in the form of access to more information and alternative sources. However, many Americans don't have access to the Internet. For many of those who do, their access is limited and controlled by large commercial providers. Furthermore, the information they obtain from these services is often just digitized versions of the same print and electric media available to the rest of us.

The concentration of media power by a few giant mega-companies also contributes to "tabloidization." As news organizations are increasingly driven by a bottom-line mentality, the news we get becomes more and more sensational.

Since my film *JFK* was released in late 1991, Congress has passed a law declassifying hundreds of thousands of pages of government documents on the subject. Nevertheless, no major newspaper, magazine or television network has devoted any resources to pursuing these leads, or to conducting a new investigation.

The media also blew an important story coming out of our *Nixon* film. The idea that Richard Nixon had been involved in assassination plots against Fidel Castro was treated as a wild "conspiracy theory" by most of the mainstream press. In fact, this has been discussed and documented by respected historians like Arthur Schlesinger and Michael Beschloss. But the

Washington press corps, always quick to rely on clichés, was mostly too lazy to dig into the historical record.

We pride ourselves on having a "free press." But how free is it when we are given the same stories by every major media conglomerate in the country, when alternative viewpoints are not accessible to most Americans? The power to control the flow of information is the power to control the way people think. That power should not be concentrated in the hands of a few conglomerates. It belongs to all of us.

Michael Arlen

Author, Living Room War *and* Exiles.

The specter of a vast, monolithic, all-pervading media has excited intellectuals—with appropriate shudders of apprehension—for much of this century. Orwell's seductive and widely applauded false prophecy in *1984* seems fairly typical, with its vision of Big Brother and his devilish artillery of loudspeakers bombarding the hundreds of millions of cowed and demoralized proles with messages of totalitarian control. How disappointing it would have been to Orwell to observe the actual playout of this romantic drama, with the ultimate non-appearance of this vast army of proles and instead the emergence over the past several decades of a startling cacophony of market-crazed citizens all over the world, with their insistence on two-way communication and their appetite for fragmentation of broadcast authority! Will the two or three or four currently forming mega-conglomerates have the last word, shape-shifting the global citizenry (newly armed with pagers and cell-phones and Internet-friendly computers and of course 500 cable channels) back into proles? One somehow doubts it.

Andrew Jay Schwartzman

Executive director, Media Access Project.

By creating a graphic display of the growing interconnection between and among the largest media empires, the diagram may enlighten a too-complacent public about the imminence of the threat. However, the presentation is far too reassuring in its relative simplicity, downplaying at least four important factors in the corporatization of civic discourse:

• It portrays a global phenomenon from a domestic perspective. Although there are representations of a few joint ventures with international companies, News Corporation (Rupert Murdoch), Bertelsmann and several other multinationals have far more influence than the chart can suggest. For example, Murdoch appears to have made programming concessions to obtain the Chinese government's blessing for delivery of satellite programming. This may well have implications for how that government is treated in U.S. domestic reportage.

• The arbitrary but necessary selection of four companies may be misleading. The more likely scenario is movement toward a *keiretsu* of eight or ten global giants.

• By highlighting only these companies, one might get the impression that they are the largest or most important players. Not so. A case could be made that John Malone of TCI has the greatest power to control program access and distribution, certainly in the United States. Yet his cable company appears in the chart only as a player sharing interests with Time Warner in CNN.

• The diagram is technologically neutral, but technology is not neutral. Companies like Microsoft and Intel want to be cut in for a percentage of everything that is extracted from end-users by licensing the protocols for transmission and the set-top converters necessary to receive digital information in the home, school and office. Even open architecture advocates such as Sun Microsystems have their own plans for getting a piece of the action. Control of standards can easily lead to control of content.

Charles Lewis

Former producer, 60 Minutes; *founder and executive director, Center for Public Integrity.*

Generally, everyone I know in journalism can be put in one of two categories: those who fear the future and long for the good old days that never were, and those who see opportunity in the uncharted world to come. What we've been doing at the Center for Public Integrity is taking advantage of the immense hunger for substance and relevance in investigative journalism. Simply stated, we don't think this is the only map.

Nolan A. Bowie

Visiting lecturer in public policy, Harvard University.

It really doesn't make a lot of difference that these media conglomerates have different names and different external appearances, for they share values and perspectives that guarantee cloned information. It is simply the nature of the market to serve the center. Indeed, the market is great at giving consumers what they want: entertainment instead of controversy, infotainment in lieu of news. Mark Fowler, chairman of the F.C.C. during the Reagan years, defined the politics of deregulation when he said that the public interest is what the public is interested in. Now corporate mergers that used to be challenged on the ground of anti-competitive vertical integration are blithely accepted as *synergy*.

Undue media concentration obliterates the notion that there is a marketplace of ideas where different viewpoints, perspectives, opinions and ways of doing things effectively compete for public attention in the search for truth, for mobilizing public opinion or for empowering citizens to make informed decisions. There is no real choice where media concentration narrows the terms of the debate and of thinking. Thus, the legitimate consent necessary for representative democracy is manufactured.

What is really frightening about this map is what is missing. It fails to include the other half of the conglomerate world, the titans of telecommunications—AT&T, MCI, GTE, TCI, Sprint, US West, S.B.C./Pacific Telesis, Ameritech, Bell South, Bell Atlantic-NYNEX etc.—that are also converging through strategic partnerships, mergers and alliances, and with these media/information/culture producers in privatized efforts to dominate global information markets. Sometime during the next decade, we may all think alike and act alike and not even notice that once we had a choice between democracy and plutocracy.

Brian Drolet and Bob Stein

Brian Drolet is a producer and Bob Stein a founder of Voyager.

The issue raised by these four companies' control of most mass media is not primarily that the free speech of journalists and writers is being choked, or that outlets for creativity are being curtailed (which they are), it is that the power to define reality lies so thoroughly in the hands of so few, and that the interests of those few are inimical to those of the many.

"The development of new technologies does make a space for entrepreneurship..."

Some see antitrust organizing as the route to taming the beast. Why would this course be more fruitful than the attempt over the past thirty years to break up the phone or airline industries? The Jeffersonian ideals of marketplace diversity and entrepreneurial competition passed decisively into history at the beginning of the twentieth century. The development of new technologies does make a space for entrepreneurship, but it's almost immediately monopolized. This chart is horrifying, but it's old news.

Many see the Internet as the ultimate democratic tool, a technology that will confound and bring down the behemoths who are wiring its nervous system. But together these companies, along with their cousins the Bells, TCI and Microsoft, are moving to extend their control over this medium as well. It is naïve to think that the Internet by the nature of its technology will prevent this takeover. But precisely because it is not yet under their control, the Internet is a crucial battleground. Right now on the Internet, people in Bosnia or South Central Los Angeles can tell their story to the world without the interpretive censor of General Electric or *The New York Times*. Because the free flow of information threatens the ability to maintain social control, there is an ideological and political as well as an economic imperative for monopolization. The battle for the Internet is part of a much larger struggle that will be fought over phone lines and in the streets.

Bill McKibben

Author, The Age of Missing Information.

Miller and Biden have done an enormous service with this many-tentacled chart; it's one of the tiny bank of crucial images we should all hold in our heads. The next time we send out one of those deep-space probes designed to crash into someone else's civilization, we should leave out recorded greetings (did you know that the voice of Kurt Waldheim narrated the last one?) and instead etch on the side this chart, maybe the graph of spiraling carbon dioxide production, perhaps the steepening curve of population. We need to leave some explanation behind. Here on this planet, we should react to this arresting image in two complementary ways. We should, obviously, begin the arduous task of reforming the nation's—and now the world's—laws about ownership of media and corporate concentration.

Others of us are opening up another front—simply to shut out most of this poisoned flow of information. It's as if we're confronted with adulterated food. We might launch a movement against pouring rat droppings into hot dogs, but at the same time we might well stop eating them and instead write cookbooks for healthy diets, hold gardening clinics and so on.

This logic holds especially true in this case. As no one has shown more brilliantly than Miller in his essays, even if TV (which is the linchpin) were owned by various orders of saintly monks, it would by its very technological existence damage us. We get fat because we sit in front of it—that data's clear. Our civic institutions erode—in part because Cap Cities could care less about them, but mainly because that's three hours less per day that we have to be involved with anything else.

To give up on these various corporate media is not irresponsible—you can learn plenty about the world from half an hour of National Public Radio. And it is not entirely quixotic to imagine it happening. I work with a group called TV Free America that last month persuaded 3 million kids to turn off the tube for a week. By all accounts most of them enjoyed it.

Leslie Savan

Columnist, The Village Voice*; author,* The Sponsored Life.

One reason that this, the *real* world wide web, gets relative little media attention is obvious: The big media players own the media that could tell the story. The effects of GE owning NBC—like NBC's soft or nonexistent coverage of nuclear energy issues—would be notorious were it not for the courtesy censorship extended by even NBC's rivals toward a fellow conglomerate.

But the big boys also get off easy because, along with their multitudinous holdings, they own their own backlash, including the potentially bruising idea that "big is bad." In fact, that idea—along with "corporations corrupt" and "media are parasites"—has become an entertainment cliché without which the monoliths can't communicate. In Disney's sequel to *The Mighty Ducks, D2,* a kids' hockey team is morally corroded by corporate sponsorship and endorsement deals—even as Disney marketing partner Coca-Cola gets repeated product placement and the kids' return to true sports spirit is rewarded with the uniforms of the real, Disney-owned Mighty Ducks of Anaheim (who produce some of the top-selling sports merchandise of the day).

It's those sorts of multiple irony pileups that muddy the issues of corporate monopoly. They make us less likely to notice that the entertainment and news products of these few companies determine more and more of the nation's emotional grammar. As concentrated power purchases any alternative vernacular or rhythm that might appear, conglomerates begin to shape our narrative, our dreamscape, our mythopoeic ambitions—whatever you want to call it. Our collective imagination becomes another profit center for GE et al., right up there with the washing machine division and nuclear isotopes.

The accompanying map describes a sort of New Age Pangea, the continent of capitalist freedom in the post–cold war world. In this new world we have finally found the answer to the age-old religious question: Does free will exist? Of course it exists: we can have Coke or Pepsi, Nike or Reebok, stuffed animals from Warner Bros. or Disney! And to all the choices the combines offer, we can give thumbs up or thumbs down! We have the power!

"Good reporters, writers and editors are spread too thin to spend the time developing the stories that the public needs."

Walter Cronkite

Everybody knows Walter Cronkite.

Nearly every important publishing and broadcasting company today is caught up in the plague of the nineties that has swept the business world—the stockholder demand to increase profits.

Adequate profits are clearly necessary for survival, but stockholders in too many cases demand superprofits. Compliant managements play the game that stock value is the only criterion of success. In the news business, that isn't good enough. The lack of a sense of public service begins today with the ownership of too many newspapers and broadcasting companies—that is, the stockholders. Stewardship of our free press is a public service and a heavy responsibility. It should not be treated the same as the manufacture of bobby pins, or of automobiles.

But to play today's downsizing game, the boards and their executives deny to their news managers enough funding to pay for the minimum coverage necessary to serve their communities adequately. Good reporters, writers and editors are spread too thin to spend the time developing the stories that the public needs. A more responsible press can come only if the owners rededicate themselves to sound journalistic principles instead of attempting to satisfy an insatiable stock market. That's the real bottom line. We all know that journalism can require all sorts of courage. The working journalist faces those challenges every day.

It seems to me that we have the right to demand a little courage on the part of those in the seats of power—the presidents and publishers and C.E.O.s—courage to face their stockholders and impress upon them the responsibility that goes with their stewardship of our free press, the basic foundation of our democracy.

Lawrence K Grossman

Former president, NBC News and PBS; author, The Electronic Republic.

What is most remarkable about the multimedia behemoths on this map is how *little* they influence U.S. political thought and opinion. The major networks' news stars, Tom Brokaw, Peter Jennings and Dan Rather, exercise no discernible sway on how viewers vote or what they think about major issues. Documentaries exploring vital political, economic and social questions have almost entirely disappeared from the nation's TV screens. Nonfiction entertainment rather than political ideas are the TV newsmagazines' stock in trade.

The media companies are essentially in the entertainment business, rather than the information or education business. Explaining why Disney bought ABC, Michael Eisner cited "the dramatically rising global appetite for nonpolitical entertainment and sports." For media conglomerates, news is mostly a useful corporate adornment. In the global pursuit of new business, new contracts, new franchises, new licenses and new government concessions, news divisions give their parent companies special access to top public officials and influential decision-makers. As we move into the new century, we need to reshape the nation's communications policies for the digital telecommunications age. Let the media conglomerates pay a fair price for their free spectrum largesse. From now on, auction off unused commercial spectrum space. Require commercial broadcasters to pay modest license fees for their valuable radio and TV frequencies. They've already benefited from the greatest giveaway of publicly owned resources in history, the free distribution of the nation's airwaves for commercial use.

A portion of the billions of dollars that can come from new spectrum revenues should be used to create a properly financed public telecommunications trust fund that would connect homes, schools, libraries, museums and government facilities in a great new interactive public service telecommunications network system. This could produce meaningful journalism, stimulate informed public discussion, deliver lifelong learning, commission quality children's programs, offer job retraining, even provide culture and the arts to all. We should also adopt today's equivalent of the land-grant colleges act of 1862, using the billions of dollars raised through spectrum auctioning to make higher education available to all who qualify. We can create an antidote to the huge media conglomerates, a vibrant new public sphere that will serve the needs of a civilized society and a vigorous democracy in the century ahead.

The Real Dangers of Conglomerate Control[2]

In media circles, the 1996 Word of the Year was "synergy." Again. Ever since the summer of 1995, when Disney's chief, Michael Eisner, embraced the term during his company's purchase of Capital Cities/ABC for some $19 billion—"The synergies are under every rock we turn over," he bubbled at one point—it's been the buzzword of choice for executives seeking to describe the dazzling possibilities for power, profit, and prestige they see as they make the leap from large company to enormous conglomerate.

But "synergy" also has been the buzzword of choice for many journalists and other observers to describe the possibilities for difficulty and danger they see in this headlong rush toward conglomeration. As more and more news organizations are bought by companies whose primary business has never been anything remotely resembling journalism—many of them companies with profit interests in such global businesses as aviation, nuclear power, financial services, sports teams, hazardous waste disposal, and other favorite targets of nosy journalists—commentators have taken to using "synergy" as a synonym for everything from "a worrisome potential for censorship" to "the death of journalism as we know it."

In November, the *Columbia Journalism Review* devoted a special breakfast forum to exploring what the consequences for journalism will be of the trend toward conglomeration. An invited group of 250 journalists, media executives, and other opinion leaders gathered to hear—and to argue with—a panel made up of four influential media critics, who presented anything but a united front in their views on the scope and seriousness of the threat to journalistic values. Moderating the panel was Ken Auletta, a longtime media critic and author who has been writing the "Annals of Communication" column for *The New Yorker* since 1992. —*Andie Tucher*

Following are excerpts from the panelists' remarks and the audience's responses.

KEN AULETTA: If you went to the press conferences when Disney took over ABC or when Westinghouse took over CBS or when Viacom took over Paramount, you heard the word synergy repeated over and over again.

Increasingly, it's also a word you hear more and more in mag-

[2] Article from the *Columbia Journalism Review* Mr/Ap '97.

azines and newspapers. People talk about the importance of enticing departments to work together, to enthuse advertisers, to get new revenues through "brand extensions." And maybe the spate of alliances that are taking place in the communications business will lead to synergy and will make journalism better. But I would argue that there's scant evidence that synergy is journalism's friend.

Let me review just a few factual arguments against synergy.

We see that in Asia Rupert Murdoch dropped the BBC from his Star satellite news service. Why? Because the BBC was offensive to the Chinese government and Rupert Murdoch and his News Corp. wanted very much to make nice to the Chinese government.

We witness the lawyers at CBS killing for a time a *60 Minutes* report on the tobacco industry. Why? Because it was deemed that CBS would face a potential lawsuit. Well, *The New York Times* faced a similar potential lawsuit, as did *The Washington Post*, with the Pentagon Papers, but the publishers decided to go forward. The argument made (in the *60 Minutes* case) was that the costs were so grave, that we shouldn't do it. I think it was really a synergy argument.

You could also make the case that a similar argument was made at ABC, when they decided to apologize, thus avoiding a potential libel award of $10 billion, to the Philip Morris Company. The question is: Was ABC's decision based on the journalistic merits? That would be, "We were wrong. We made a mistake and we're owning up to it."

Or was it a decision of corporate convenience? That would be, "We can't do anything to impede the merger of ABC and Disney." I suspect that you pick up here the scent of synergy.

Nor is synergistic thinking a stranger to the newspaper world. Take a look at what happened at the Times Mirror Company with the new C.E.O. who comes in and says, "We have to get our profit margins up from 8 percent to, eventually, 16 percent."

Well, you can make an argument that there's a lot of fat at Times Mirror. But if you talk privately to business people at the Times Mirror Company, they will tell you that there's a point at which you go beyond cutting fat, to cutting bone. Now, the truth of the matter is it's much easier to measure your costs or profit margins than it is to quantify something that's very dear to those of us in journalism, which is quality.

"...business people at the Times Mirror Company... will tell you that there's a point at which you go beyond cutting fat, to cutting bone."

As communications Goliaths merge and partner, occasions for these journalistic conflicts of interest will inevitably increase. Will ABC News aggressively cover a proposed Disney theme park on an old Civil War site? Will NBC News go easy on its online partner, Microsoft?

Did Paramount executives agree to curb the paparazzi that violate the privacy of Hollywood stars because they thought it was an outrageous intrusion of privacy? Or did they curb them because they want to make nice to stars like George Clooney and get them to do movies for Paramount? Will the *New York Post* continue to be used as a weapon by Rupert Murdoch to bludgeon political or business opponents?

Will *The New Yorker* accept too many excerpts of books from Random House, which is part of its parent company? Will *Forbes* slyly drop another profile, as they did two years ago with the agent Michael Ovitz, without telling people that Ovitz was, in fact, a private consultant to *Forbes*?

Or, conversely, is it true, as my friend Walter Isaacson at *Time* argues, that journalists are more insulated from intrusion from their corporate bosses when they work in the bosom of a large company, which is less interested in the outcome of particular stories, than they might be in a smaller one? There's some evidence of that, but I think there is a greater journalistic peril in a large conglomerate. It comes not from Jack Welch, the head of General Electric, reaching down and saying. "Do this story." It comes from self-censorship, from anticipatory censorship. People saying, "God! If we run this story, will it ruin our careers? Will we be labeled non-team players?"

Witness, for instance, how NBC issued an apology after Bob Costas made a perfectly reasonable statement on the network during the Olympics about human rights abuses in China. An NBC spokesman, a couple of days later, issued the following statement, speaking about China, "We wanted to make it clear that we didn't intend to hurt their feelings." Now, presumably. NBC also didn't want to hurt the business interests of the corporate parent, General Electric, which is bidding for business in China.

Inevitably, the synergy notion produces a clash of values between the corporate culture of the parent and the culture of journalism. The new mega-corporations in the communications world value things like teamwork. They use leverage to boost sales of their products. They dream of a borderless company that eliminates the defensive interior barriers and walls within those companies.

But journalists are meant to prize their independence, not teamwork. To keep a distance from advertisers, not to seek synergies with them. Journalists need borders. That is to say, a degree of independence, in order to do our jobs. Journalists don't aspire to a borderless company, because we want to keep the business and the advertising department the hell out of the news room. That's part of our mission.

So the more corporate retreats you invite editors to, the more the danger you have of converting those editors into tame, corporate citizens. This, of course, often gets complicated and there are other sides to this argument. Only paranoids, for instance, want editors to be implacable foes of the publishers.

And it is true that journalism is a business, not a philanthropic activity. If you don't make money, as *New York Newsday* didn't make money, you should be closed no matter how good a product you produce.

One can make the argument that media conglomerates will restrict the information we receive, that we citizens will be victims of a homogenized, commercial sameness. There is plenty of evidence that entertainment values have infected our business. Perhaps you saw the Diane Sawyer interview with Fergie, as they call her at ABC News. It was an entire hour of what used to be documentary time, devoted to a one-hour interview with the Duchess of York.

But one could also argue the opposite, that George Orwell was wrong, that technology will not imprison us, will not become a tool for totalitarian governments or for big companies. Instead, as happened in Eastern Europe, with the introduction of fax machines and satellite and cellular phones, borders and Berlin Walls were proved to be porous.

The Chinese can talk about controlling the Internet. But they will not be able to do it. Meanwhile, back at home, the questions arise: Need we fear the concentration of media power? Is bigness journalism's enemy, or its own enemy? Will more sources of news equal more choice or more infotainment?

We'll try to identify now the poison.

Auletta's remarks were followed by comment from:

Frank Rich, an op-ed columnist and former theater critic for *The New York Times*;

Dorothy Rabinowitz, media columnist for *The Wall Street Journal* and a member of the *Journal*'s editorial board;

Alex Jones, the host of National Public Radio's *On the Media*, who won a 1987 Pulitzer Prize for his *New York Times* reports on the fall of the Bingham newspaper dynasty in Louisville, Kentucky; and

Howard Kurtz, media reporter for *The Washington Post* and the author most recently of *Hot Air: All Talk, All the Time*.

FRANK RICH: This summer I was on vacation in Italy. And about three days after I arrived there, I suddenly turned to my wife and said, "I realize that something is different about this culture, in addition to all the other things that are different about Italy." And it was that there was no palpable Disney presence.

If you believe, as I do, that culture is also news, this consolidation of power in a handful of companies not only affects whether stories about Philip Morris run, or whether there's coverage of the telecom bill—which there essentially was not—when it was before Congress. It also affects the whole air we breathe. In terms of what we all call synergy. Because these companies disseminate their products in every possible outlet. And it really affects our values, what we think of as our culture

And, while there is this explosion of news sources, in terms of the Web, I still don't think we know where that's going to all lead.

DOROTHY RABINOWITZ: As long as I've been a journalist, there have been these dark, threatening phantoms looming before us, threatening to undermine journalistic independence and integrity. This time it is synergism. But I think that the enemy of journalism remains what it always was.

The enemy has always been the herd mentality, the wish not to step out of line with the prevailing moral order. It isn't synergy or the threat of conglomerates that is causing reporters everywhere to report a story in lock-step, with tremendous fear of offending—you know the overused term—political correctness.

I don't remember any golden age of journalism. There was a fellow at *The Washington Star* who had lurched over to *The Washington Times*. Then, when the Reverend Sun Myung Moon bought the *Times* somebody asked him, "Isn't it going to be terrible that you're going to be working for the Reverend Sun Myung Moon?" And he answered, "I don't know. As long as I've been in journalism, I never met a publisher who didn't think he was God."

Let us deal with the demons that are here before us in journalism that have always been here. And worry less about these varying threats to the perceived independence of journalists.

ALEX JONES: At the turn of the century, people were anxious about concentrations of power, just the way they are today. But the concentrations they were more worried about were the insurance trusts and the railroads, and the embodiment of that sort of thing was J.P. Morgan. Americans have a deep, visceral fear of that sort of power. When you start trying to crack why people are saying the things they do about the media these days, one aspect of it is pure visceral anxiety about a creature that they feel they have no real way to control. Something that has become vastly powerful, something that is to a large degree faceless.

The leading news organs in this country are the TV networks, and those networks are now divisions of branches of subsidiaries. In other words, the people who control the most important news outlets in this country have absolutely no understanding or value for news and journalism values. That has never been true before. There's another kind of pernicious aspect to this. And that is the sense that we all have that even though there's a huge amount of competition and rivalry with Time Warner and News Corp. and Condé Nast and Viacom and Bill Gates and John Malone and Dow Jones, that it's one large corporation. Because they are now not only becoming these synergistic creatures unto themselves but they are also forming alliances that are making them one. And Americans viscerally and intellectually, rationally sense that. Do I find it a disturbing concept? Yes, I certainly and very much do.

HOWARD KURTZ: It's important that we not mythologize the nonexisting good old days because it is obviously true that people like Mr. Hearst and Mr. Pulitzer were also interested in making money. In this age when I can think of myself as a content provider instead of just an aging hack, a more important point to me—rather than will NBC aggressively cover General Electric, because there always will be somebody to blow the whistle on malfeasance at General Electric—is whether these companies are willing to spend money. Spend real serious resources on news. I surf the Web a lot, and go onto these sites that have got all these great bells and whistles and interactivity. But what you don't see on most of these sites is much or any original reporting.

One of the reasons for that is reporting is expensive. Investigative reporting is expensive. Why? Because you spend weeks, months, gathering documents. Sometimes the story doesn't pan out. It requires not only an investment, but a commitment to doing serious journalism. And it is risky, in terms of lawsuits and the threat of lawsuits. When you do original, aggressive enterprise reporting, you step on powerful toes.

So, it is certainly true that we are now moving into an age where we will have more choices of news than ever before. But in watching some of the new cable channels that are coming online, I see a lot of talk, a lot of analysis, a lot of opinion, a lot of blather. I don't see that much newsgathering. Because newsgathering is very expensive.

We don't have to speculate about how ABC will cover Disney. We have a real live example that occurred just a few weeks ago when *Good Morning America* devoted most of its two hours to a show in, about, and celebrating Disney World's twenty-fifth anniversary.

Charlie Gibson and Joan Lunden and the whole crew went down to Orlando at great expense and, just to give you the tone of this hard-hitting report, here is some of what was said:

Joan Lunden—"Disney World rocks around the clock.... The attention to detail in this place is really astounding."

Charlie Gibson—"Probably the greatest man-made vacation center that has ever been built."

Joan Lunden—"Just another example of going all out to impress even the most hard-to-please visitors."

And then of course, there was the obligatory interview with Disney C.E.O. Michael Eisner. I asked Charlie Gibson about it and he was candid enough to say "I'd be lying to you if I didn't say there were some people who weren't comfortable about it."

Notice the careful phrase "some people" leaving open the possibility of whether that included him. This was as close to an infomercial as I have ever seen on network television. Perhaps if it had been by some other network that wasn't owned by Disney it would just have been in poor taste but I thought it was something more serious.

RICH: We're still at the beginning of this phenomenon. A company like ABC still has producers in ABC News who came out of what we think of as a journalistic tradition. A magazine like *Time* still has a number of the same editors who were working there when I was there long before it became Time Warner. But these people are going to retire, fade away. And the question is, will people who come in be people who have no institutional memory of what journalism is or journalistic values? Will there be a whole new kind of nonjournalistic employee who comes out of a corporate culture where everything is about publicity? Because that's what synergy is.

KURTZ: We have the convergence of two important developments. One is bigger and bigger companies getting involved in the news business. That is probably not so different except in degree from what we've seen in the past century. The other is the speed of the news cycle, which now seems permanently stuck on fast forward.

"...the speed of the news cycle... now seems permanently stuck on fast forward."

Those two things are important because one of the reasons you have people filling up the air time with not terribly insightful blather is that there's a lot of air time to fill. And there is less and less time and in some cases less and less inclination for what we used to think of as sort of the mainstream, old-line traditional—some would say dinosaur—news organizations to check out these stories that get into this media culture from a hundred different sources. A story about O.J. can start on an L.A. TV station and rocket around the world and be in newspapers and be on the Internet in a matter of hours before anybody happens to know whether it's true or not.

So some of the safeguards that we used to have that made us slow, that probably made us elitists, have vanished. Now there's a good side to that because it means that more voices come into the conversation. But there's also a dangerous side to it.

JONES: The press's problem is not enough resources and not enough corporate will and not enough real leadership in newsrooms.

I'm not talking about *The Washington Post* and *The Wall Street Journal* and so forth. But at small newspapers around the country there are executives and editors who are simply not allowed to lead their newsrooms in ways that are going to be threatening to the interests of the bottom line.

Journalists are among the most idealistic and driven people in American society. There's a real crisis of confidence and in morale among journalists now because they feel they're not being led right. They're simply not being told that they're doing something really important and they're not being allowed to do many of the things that brought them into journalism in the first place.

The panelists' remarks were followed by questions and comments from the floor—and responses from the panel.

GUEST: I cannot recall a time when big business and powerful interests were more scrutinized by the press than now. NBC may not want to take on General Electric but CBS and ABC will do so without any question. My point is journalism is still free and competition for news makes almost any powerful interest vulnerable. But when I was a reporter we had sacred top cows; we never reported an elevator accident in a large department store that advertised.

GUEST: There's a piece of this synergism that you left out. That's the relationship between the corporations and the government and their dependence on government contracts, particularly military. The public perception is that the media are now p.r. people for the government. That's where a lot of the cynicism comes from.

GUEST: We are letting ourselves off much too lightly. Every anecdote, every incident that was mentioned today—except perhaps for Murdoch and the BBC—represents a real terrible failure of nerve and duty by the journalists. Are we using this corporate stuff as a scapegoat for bad journalism and nerveless journalism?

JONES: The only people in the broadcast news departments who have any real power are the stars. They're also enormously paid, so they have an enormous vested interest in not rocking a boat.

But they are the only ones who really have the power to embarrass or to shame a network news operation into doing something that it does not feel is in its interest to do. It's not really going to matter in many of those operations whether the news director resigns. If Mike Wallace had walked off, it would have made a big difference. I think this is going to put a great deal of pressure on these star journalists to be the ones who put themselves on the line when journalistic crises come along.

KURTZ: Let me dissent slightly. I think that a lot of journalists in the trenches do have the power to just say no. There is always the threat that somebody in that position can go public and cause an awful lot of bad publicity, which media companies hate as intensely if not more intensely than other types of companies. The fact is that if more of us would blow the whistle rather than just blaming the big, bad corporate owners, then some of these excesses would be curbed.

Corporate Influence Makes Sure You'll Never Get to See This Show[3]

On the evening of April 22, when we came to the intercessions at our Fordham Jesuit community Mass, one of the fathers announced that "at this moment" the Peruvian army was laying siege to the Japanese Embassy in Lima and that we should pray for everyone involved.

I almost jumped up and checked out of Mass to catch the assault on CNN. Here was TV news at its best. How could I afford to miss it?

But I stuck to my prayers and waited for "Nightline" for the "big picture" on what had happened. I had been to Peru during the election campaign that mysteriously brought Alberto K. Fujimori to power, and I have followed what has happened to that dazzlingly beautiful country with a mixture of confusion and sadness.

So, "Nightline." Boom! Boom! There go the government troops. There go the hostages scampering to freedom. There's Fujimori in a flak jacket wielding a gun, on the scene within minutes, gloating over his wipeout. Fujimori for president of the United States! Here's a real decision-maker. Statistics: only two dead assault troops and only one dead hostage (no word on who killed him). All 14 rebels killed. Now to our analysis: wonderful. Masterful. The rest of us have something to learn about how to handle terrorists like a champ.

Call it the give-it-a-week syndrome. That means: With any sensational news story don't believe it till a week's follow-up has given us a better picture. Look closely at a picture in Thursday's *New York Daily News* of the shirtless corpse of a rebel and you'll notice that the boy has no head.

By Sunday we know the answers to the questions that Tuesday's "Nightline" should have asked. The evidence indicates that Fujimori ordered his troops to execute all the captors, including those who refused to execute their hostages and tried to surrender. Then chop them up.

As Clarence Page said on Sunday's "McLaughlin Group," to the guffaws of his co-panelists, Fujimori's is a "state terrorist government," and the rebels have a case that isn't getting much attention in the American press.

By then, National Public Radio's "Newsweek on the Air" and *The New York Times* had broadcast and published analyses and

---

[3] Article by Raymond A. Schroth, Jesuit Father and assistant dean of Fordham College and author of *The American Journey of Eric Sevareid*, from *National Catholic Reporter* May 16, '97.

letters indicating that the rebels' main "failure" was that they were not ruthless enough. Like the Latin American teenagers they were, they liked to lay down they weapons and take off their shirts and play soccer—which gave the Peruvian army in the tunnels a chance to blow them up. They died having killed no one, and their families were not allowed to see their corpses—lest we have evidence on how they died.

Which brings us to "Fear and Favor in the Newsroom," a powerful documentary collection of recent case studies, produced by California Newsreel..., in which some of the nation's best journalists are cut off from doing their jobs—giving us the information we need in order to make wise political judgments.

Unfortunately, however, the only people who know about "Fear and Favor" are those who heard it discussed on Alex Jones' "On the Media," on New York Public Radio's WNYC, or caught its one New York showing, with a panel discussion, at New York University in March.

These stories offend local and national corporations, which share directorships with the corporate owners of the media, corporate sponsors on whom public TV depends, and the government, which control the press' access to a story like the Gulf War.

As far as I know, Peru's and Fujimori's corporate backers don't own ABC, but establishment TV news programs never care about "enemy" dead or how they died. It is presumed their deaths are good news because "we won." To consider that they died because "our side" didn't want to deal with the questions surrendered rebels might raise in court, if they could get a trial, was not allowed.

The case studies in "Fear and Favor" are familiar to anyone who has been reading for the past few years the *Columbia Journalism Review* or *The Nation*—particularly *The Nation*'s special June 3, 1996, issue documenting corporate media control. But the film's extraordinary power comes from the authority of its voices.

These are no mere disgruntled amateurs teed off at their editors for not getting their way, but some of America's best journalists, prizewinners trying to do their jobs but thwarted by a newsroom culture in which management freezes out stories that make trouble and editors are supposed to think profits as well as news.

• When *New York Times* alumnus Bill Kovach took over the *Atlanta Journal-Constitution* (owned by the Cox Corporation) in 1986, his reporters published an exposé of Atlanta banks that wouldn't make loans in black neighborhoods and even criticized the local god, the Coca Cola Corporation, which was under investigation by a grand jury.

It happened that a Coke executive was on the *Constitution*'s board. In two years Kovach, who in the words of reporter Bill Dedman had inspired his staff to believe that under his leadership they would be able to "barbecue the sacred cows," was gone, and the *Constitution* published five days of soft "news" kissing up to Coke.

• When *The New York Times'* Frances Cerra exposed the billion-dollar cost overruns in the Long Island Shoreham nuclear plant and her findings contradicted the *Times'* editorial policy, she was taken off the story and soon left the paper.

• When Peter Praumann reported a story in 1992 for the PBS "MacNeil/Lehrer Newshour" on the disposal of nuclear waste, producers cut the footage on hazards inherent in storage of the waste and on the danger of its leaking into streams all over the country. According to this documentary there have been two virtual Chernobyls—almost-meltdowns—since Three Mile Island in 1979. Only CBS News noticed—with a quick, soundbite report on one.

• When *New York Times* Pulitzer Prize winner Sydney Schanberg, hero of *The Killing Fields,* pointed out in his op-ed page column that the New York press had not sufficiently reported the corruption involved in the Westway project, a plan to develop Manhattan's West Side bordering the Hudson River, the *Times* ownership told him he had gone too far and yanked his column.

Schanberg left the paper for which he had risked his life and won a Pulitzer covering the war in Cambodia. He joined *New York Newsday,* until its owner, the *Los Angeles Times,* closed it to save a few bucks two years ago. Today, one of America's best journalists is waiting for an assignment that will let him both use his skills and keep his ideals.

It's important to realize that one can write weak, embarrassing, narrow-minded columns for the *Times'* op-ed page for years. But one may not, even implicitly, criticize the *Times.* As *Times* vice-president Sydney Gruson—one of the few targets willng to defend his decisions on camera—put it, this was too much.

• When *The Wall Street Journal*'s Jonathan Kwitny's PBS investigative program tied U.S. corporations in with the repressive government in Guatemala, his corporate funding dried up and he lost his program. Meanwhile, Kwitny observes, John McLaughlin, who says exactly what corporate America wants us all to hear, has sailed along with three programs on which to say whatever he pleases.

"Fear and Favor" reminds us—lest we forget—of the ways in which the cheerleader alliance between the government and the establishment media made it difficult for Americans to get a just appraisal of the Gulf War. Again, Hooray for the Boom! Boom! Boom!

The night sky over Baghdad lights up like "a hundred Fourth of Julys," says ABC's Peter Jennings as George Bush launches his rescue operation on behalf of the Kuwaiti royal family. When reporter John Alpert was the first to get film footage documenting the toll of American bombing on Iraq's civilian population, NBC refused to use it. Alpert was a "man with a mission," says

NBC news president Michael Gartner, so his report was not to be trusted. But subsequent reporting bore out the truth of his story.

Media scholar Ben Bagdikain, author of *The Media Monopoly*, the classic study of how the concentration of media power shrinks free speech, provides a Greek chorus of running commentary, along with Studs Terkel's narration. So, with an all-star cast, why haven't we seen "Fear and Favor in the Newsroom" on our home screens?

Well, PBS can't run it because it twits MacNeil/Lehrer and PBS's subservience to corporate sponsors. *The New York Times* won't write about it, because it embarrasses the *Times*. And those are the good guys! Arts and Entertainment Network? Maybe they might. They've run media critiques before. But this one comes from the "left"; this one presumes that the purpose of the press is to make powerful people—in government, business or the media—behave by criticizing them, by threatening them with exposure.

Yes, there are legitimate journalistic principles that justify keeping "Fear and Favor" off the air. It's "advocacy" journalism with a clear point of view. It's "old news," a repackaging of previously published material to foster a "liberal" point: Corporate media ownership silences open discussion.

But corporate journalism, too, is "advocacy"—by freezing out the "bad" news we need to know. It breeds "old news" the mainstream audience never gets to read and see, or—like the image of the corpse of the headless rebel in Lima—sees long after the public mood has been set. Then it's too late.

The Corporatization of Publishing[4]

The mighty heads of America's conglomerate publishers, as well as a group of the small independent editors, converged on Paris in late March at the invitation of the French government. The United States was the theme of the Paris Book Fair, and it was clear that the invitations had been arranged as if for a Feydeau bedroom farce. As the major players left from one salon door, the small independent publishers were ushered into another; the possibility of confrontation, discussion or debate was carefully avoided. The polarized U.S. publishing scene was represented accurately, but its extremes remained as separate as ever.

For the French, this polarization was no doubt a difficult concept to grasp. While the conglomerates there control some 60 percent of the publishing industry as a whole, the intellectual scene is still dominated by the traditional, family-owned and serious publishers. Even the conglomerates find they have to vie for sales and respectability by keeping to a program that includes books many an American university press would envy.

For the rest of the continent, publishing is still close to what we had in the United States twenty years ago. The large media companies have not yet taken over all the major houses; the profits expected from books are not yet those expected from film or television; and the bookstores are still filled with a wide variety of books, political and literary, that have long disappeared from most of ours. How has U.S. publishing come to resemble the mass media in so short a time? The changes that have taken place in our media culture during my professional life are so vast that it is hard to comprehend fully how extensive they have been.

I started out in publishing in the late fifties working for a mass paperback house with the ungainly name of the New American Library of World Literature. Its slogan was "Good Reading for the Millions." Although N.A.L. published *Forever Amber* and other pulp fiction of its time, and its executives were certainly concerned with sales and profit, it still made available some of the best contemporary writing at the lowest price. Books were distributed throughout the country not simply through bookstores but through cigar stores, drug stores and the like, where for 25 cents (then the price of a pack of cigarettes) Americans had access to Faulkner, Kerouac, Pratolini or the young Mailer; to Margaret Mead's *Coming of Age in Samoa* and to Marquis Childs's *Sweden: The Middle Way on Trial.*

While the *Forever Ambers* were necessary to pay the bills,

[4] Article by André Schiffrin, former managing director of Pantheon Books and founder of The New Press, a non-for-profit publisher in NY, from *The Nation*, June 3, 1996.

N.A.L. was determined to make available a very wide choice. The ideology, and it was an ideology, was that the general population should have access to the best of the world's culture. This policy began in the heady days of the thirties, when the New Deal was dominant, and carried on through World War II, when free copies of many of these books were given to U.S. servicemen. Publishing "good reading for the millions" was a conscious, deliberate effort.

Today, if you visit any airport newsstand, you will see that the books featured are the top best sellers, plus a few other titles by popular authors. The titles I've mentioned—or their contemporary equivalents—are for the most part unavailable in those outlets, and they are available elsewhere only because some university press or small alternative publisher has re-published them, often at a high price.

"...market ideology has been accompanied by legislation that has increasingly changed the nature of book publishing."

We have seen in recent years the application of market theory to the dissemination of culture. Spurred by the Thatcher/Reagan changes in politics, the owners of publishing houses rationalize their policies by invoking the market. It is not up to elites to impose their values on readers, they claim; it is up to the public to choose what it wants—and if what it wants is bad, so be it. Houses with histories as distinguished as Knopf have not hesitated to take on books so perverse and violent, like *American Psycho*, that they have been turned away by other conglomerates. The question is which books will make the most money, not which ones will fulfill the publisher's traditional cultural mission.

The development of the market ideology has been accompanied by legislation that has increasingly changed the nature of book publishing. In both the United States and Britain, funding for libraries has been drastically cut. There was a time in both countries when library purchases were large enough to cover much of the costs of serious fiction and nonfiction.

The editorial process has also been skewed by the fact that at large companies, decisions about what to publish are made not by editors but by so-called publishing committees, in which the financial and marketing people play a pivotal role. If a book does not look as if it will sell a certain number—and that number increases with every year—these people argue that the company cannot "afford" to take it on, especially when it is a new novel or a work of serious nonfiction. What the Spanish newspaper *El País* perceptively called "market censorship" is increasingly in force in a decision-making process that is based on whether there is a pre-existing audience for any book. The obvious success and the well-known author are the books now sought; new authors and new, critical viewpoints are increasingly finding it difficult to be published in the major houses.

Obviously, new ideologies do not develop out of thin air. They are part of the *Zeitgeist* but they are also part of a new structure, in this case the rise of the large international conglomerates. Increasing concentration has brought with it a drive for dramatic increases in profits. Since the twenties, through prosperity and depression, the average profit for all publishing houses has been around 4 percent after taxes. This includes both the houses that were intensely commercial and sought (even then) to publish only those books they felt to be eminently profitable, as well as the important houses that we all recall as forming the culture of our time, houses that sought to balance profitability with responsibility. The owners of these latter houses, the Alfred A. Knopfs and others, did not retire in poverty. But they were happy to have the value of their house grow gradually from year to year; they did not bleed it each year of the capital necessary for the maintenance of its list.

It is instructive to look at the current figures for those European houses that have not yet been corporatized. In France, the most prestigious of the traditional publishing houses, Gallimard, makes an annual profit of a little over 3 percent, despite what is probably the strongest backlist in Europe and a flourishing and imaginative children's book section. Le Seuil, probably the second most impressive of the French houses, came up last year with a profit of just over 1 percent. At this moment, both houses are still owned by the founding families and their allies.

In the United States and Britain, where more and more independent houses are being taken over by conglomerates, the new owners have insisted that the profitability of the book publishing arm should be similar to the high returns they demand from other subsidiaries like newspapers, cable television and film. New profit targets have therefore been established in the range of 12 to 15 percent.

To meet these new expectations, publishers have drastically changed the nature of what they publish. The "smaller books"—serious fiction, art history, criticism—have all but disappeared from the lists of the major houses. The emphasis has been shifted to pay huge advances for what are hoped to be huge best sellers. But since every other major house has been following the same policy, advances increasingly go beyond what is reasonable to expect a book will earn These huge advances are written off, vast losses are incurred and the publisher must cut back even more, eliminating the "midlist" and taking away from the smaller books what is left for marketing and advertising in order to try once again with a Jeffrey Archer or a Danielle Steele. Indeed, recent layoffs at HarperCollins in London have been reported in the British press as being a direct result of the enormous (and unearned) £32 million advance (close to $50 million) paid to Archer.

Needless to say, not all the houses are able to make their profit targets. Indeed, there are reports that some of the large corporations are far less profitable than they were five years ago, when they were pursuing their traditional and diversified policy. But if one house succeeds, all the others are told they must try harder. If someone does make 15 percent in a year, the others are expected to do the same, and the unfortunate front-runner is then expected to make 16 percent. One of the most interesting lessons, yet one of the hardest to learn, is that there is no such thing as enough when such unrealistic profit targets are set. Newhouse, for instance, bought the Random House empire for some $60 million. Ten years later, his holdings had increased in value to over $1 billion. But this did not suffice. Greater annual profits were expected of each of the publishing units, so each of the houses changed its list accordingly, until the group as a whole had altered its character completely.

"We have no idea what kind of money will be charged for access to information in the future."

The story of the Reed Elsevier group, which owns, in addition to trade publishing houses, *Publishers Weekly*, reference book publishers and other media properties, is typical. Some of its units make as much as 30 percent a year, and they too are required to show plans for the annual increase of their profits. After buying up some of England's most distinguished publishing houses—Methuen, Heinemann, Secker & Warburg—Reed announced in August 1995 that it intended to sell them off because they simply could not make their targets. Generally when such companies are bought, their assets are stripped, their backlist merged into a common paperback list, their editors dismissed, many of their authors urged to depart. What is left to sell after this process is relatively little, and confirms in the minds of the new owners that publishing is not the investment they once thought it to be. The other week, Reed announced that it had found no takers and would continue its trade publishing program. The price that its staff and authors have paid for months of uncertainty and despair can easily be imagined. In the end, profitability of the Reed publishing entity was reported to be 12 percent. A double irony then—the profit that many houses in the United States and England are pursuing without success is deemed to be insufficient to those who have even more profitable investments.

Reed executives decided that instead of investing in traditional publishing ("consumer publishing," as they elegantly called it), they would concentrate on the new field of information retrieval. More and more publishers are talking about concentrating on the profitable tip of the information pyramid, making available on computers and through other electronic media the information that used to be available simply by consulting a book. We have no idea what kind of money will be charged for access to information in the future. But it is a danger signal that many of those planning this shift see it as one of great profit potential. There is growing concern that public libraries and other free, open institutions will have less and less access to information, and will be charged for information that used to be available without charge.

Another pressure on publishing is rising overheads. Publishing used to pay relatively low salaries. Editors earned roughly what a professor would, assistant editors roughly what a lecturer would and so on. Now publishers have raised their salaries to phenomenal heights, reaching into the millions. A recent *PW* survey shows the head of McGraw-Hill to be making more than $1.5 million a year more than the head of Exxon or Philip Morris.

One of the side-effects of corporatization is the increasing intent of book publishers to mimic the lifestyles of their colleagues in Hollywood. Publishers' offices become more and more showy, resembling banks rather than the offices of their predecessors; salaries and expense accounts have risen accordingly. The sales conferences at Random House were costing a million dollars each—twice a year—by the time I left. These overheads must be paid for even before the annual profits are declared. The reason so many publishers claim they cannot afford to publish a book that will sell fewer than 15,000 or 20,000 copies is not that the book cannot break even at those numbers. The reason is that each book must throw off a certain contribution to overhead, often $100,000 or more, to justify its place on the list.

These internal demands are part of the transformation of the ideology of publishing. When people can no longer be proud of the books they publish, and justify their own careers by the books they have brought into the world, the cruder rewards of money and status are needed to fill the moral gap.

The third basic change is a political one. It can best be illustrated by a recent event. Basic Books, the prestigious social science publisher now owned by HarperCollins, published a biography of Deng Xiaoping, by his daughter. It is badly written, full of excuses and lacking information—the kind of book that no Western publisher would look at twice under normal circumstances. But not only was the book published by Basic, it was launched with a massive publicity campaign, reported to have cost at least $100,000, in which the author was brought from China and presented to the press and public. Why was so much effort devoted to this book? For one thing, Rupert Murdoch, who owns HarperCollins, was eager to obtain from the Chinese government permission for his Sky cable network to broadcast in China. He had already agreed to censor the network so that the BBC News would be blocked, but those assurances, apparently, were not sufficient to get the contract for hire. A little additional persuasion was needed—*voilà*, the publication of this embarrassing volume.

To Murdoch, the use of publishing to obtain greater ends is simply part of business as usual. A great deal of press attention was paid to the initial proposal by HarperCollins to pay Newt Gingrich an advance of $4.5 million. The book's sales now look as if they will earn, at the very most, a third of that. Even with the promise of a paperback sale and a second book, it is clear that the amount first offered the Representative exceeded any reasonable expectation of what sales might be. Under the circumstances, Murdoch's eagerness to consult Gingrich on the fate of his immensely valuable TV franchises, even before the contract had been signed, becomes even more telling.

In the United States, the political nature of books has changed drastically since the conglomerates acquired so many houses. Harper, Random House and Simon & Schuster were once bastions of New Deal liberalism. Yet the current output of U.S. publishing is markedly to the right. The editors involved are still basically the same people; one must assume that they are responding to new pressures. Indeed, one of the major reasons my colleagues and I left Pantheon after all those years was the clear directive from the new Random House management that we should move away from the kind of political publishing for which Pantheon had been known, that we should consider books from the right instead. Random House, of course, denied afterward that it had made any such statements. But one has only to look at the Random House lists five years later to see the degree to which it has abandoned critical political and social commentary, and instead publishes authors from the right.

The same thing is happening throughout the publishing industry. In a recent survey of new political books, *Publishers Weekly* listed some forty titles, all essentially from the right with the exception of two—one from The New Press and one from the Brookings Institution, both nonprofit publishers. Left-of-center books are now primarily published by small independent and alternative houses, such as Beacon, South End and others.

Now of course the larger houses will say that those decisions are market-driven. But it is hard to argue that there are no readers open to alternative views. Indeed, the marked success of The New Press's own recent books dealing with politics confirms both the substantial nature of the audience and the need for publishers to play a countercyclical role. Books on political issues, particularly in election years, were for many years traditional fare of U.S. publishing houses. Yet in 1992, during the presidential election, there were virtually no books published for the general reader dealing with the major issues facing American citizens—NAFTA, national health insurance, the future of the welfare system—other than those taking a right-wing viewpoint, often subsidized by conservative foundations and then published by major conglomerates.

The problems of publishing have been exacerbated by the rise of major bookstore chains, which to a large degree share the profit-centered ideology of the media conglomerates. The major chains focus their energies and very considerable resources on the best sellers. Bookselling has been divided by a civil war in which independent bookstores claim they are constantly threatened by the chains, which have an aggressive policy of opening new stores close to successful independents. As a result, more and more independents go out of business; in the center of New

York City it is difficult to find more than a handful—that number has been diminished by three in recent months.

In a series of lawsuits brought by the American Booksellers Association, the independents have charged that the large publishers favor the chains through unfair practices. These publishers pay large amounts of so-called "co-op" advertising money to be sure best sellers are advantageously placed in the stores. Smaller publishers, taking a gamble on a less accessible book, are hard put to pay the extra co-op money, and the chances of their books being stocked in any quantity diminish accordingly.

What reversals of these trends are possible? The only major changes that could come would be by the strict application of antitrust laws in the United States and Great Britain—the very laws that have been waived to allow media conglomerates like Murdoch's to gain ever-increasing power. Political leaders are wary of opposing those who control the media, and have been quick to give way to the demands.

"There is a new generation of young publishers willing to take on the 'commercially incorrect'..."

It would be unrealistic at this point to expect either Clinton or the Republicans to challenge the major media conglomerates head-on. But this does not mean that no Congressional action is possible. Not many years ago Senator Paul Simon and others organized hearings on concentration in the media, supported by author groups such as PEN, then far more politically daring. Should no member of Congress be willing to run the considerable risks of taking on the media giants, citizen hearings, teach-ins and other tools are available. The most dangerous aspect of the current increase in conglomerate power is that it has gone largely unchallenged, that antitrust legislation is not even discussed, that other forms and structures of media ownership are hardly contemplated.

Another opportunity is the proliferation of small, independent houses. These are growing in the United States. Though their names—Dalkey Archive, Graywolf Press, Verso Books, Thunder's Mouth, Milkweed, etc.—are still largely unknown to the public, from them come a wide variety of serious and important books. In a vast cultural desert, the combined effort of all the independent presses does succeed in making a few flowers bloom. But only a few. The share of the market of these presses is minuscule, at most 1 percent of total book sales. Moreover, they do not have the strength or resources of the major firms, and do not have anywhere near as ready an access to bookstores.

The problem overall is a political and economic one. Until governments feel strong enough to challenge the power of the enormous conglomerates, the solutions that can be offered will have to be partial. Still, these new alternatives offer us the beginnings of choice. There is a new generation of young publishers willing to take on the "commercially incorrect" and, particularly in fiction and poetry, these new houses have come close to replacing their older and larger competitors.

When my colleagues and I left Pantheon in 1990 rather than decimate its list and completely transform its character, I was approached by a number of people offering venture capital, or an imprint in one of the larger houses. But it seemed to me that a new kind of structure was needed to deal with this very different publishing scene—a new, not-for-profit form of publishing. And so we formed The New Press, which has the structure of a university press without university ownership. It seeks to reach the broadest of audiences with serious political, social and cultural work, and in the first four years, publishing some 150 books, we have learned that the audiences are clearly there.

The drive for profit that determines capitalism at the end of this century fits like an iron mask on our cultural output. Unlike Europe, we have lost most of the remnants of nineteenth-century capitalism, the family-owned firms whose owners could decide whether or not to maximize profit. If we were talking about similar changes in other industries, the results might not be as dangerous. If a few international manufacturers of clothing offer us an ever-more-limited choice of jeans, the culture is not deeply threatened. But if we have purveyors of culture who feel that one idea can fit all, then not only our future but our very ability to debate what it should be will be at risk.

Bibliography

An asterisk (*) preceding a reference indicates that an excerpt from the work has been reprinted in this compilation or that the work has been cited.

Books and Pamphlets

Clinard, Marshall Barron. Corporate corruption: the abuse of power. Praeger '90.

Erve, Marc van der. Power of tomorrow's management. Butterworth-Heinemann '93.

* Fallows, James M. Breaking the news: how the media undermine American democracy. Vintage '97.

Felstead, Alan. The corporate paradox: power and control in the business franchise. Routledge '93.

* Frank, Thomas C. Conglomerates and the media. The New Press '97.

Grefe, Edward A. and Linsky, Martin. The new corporate activism: harnessing the power of grassroots tactics for your organization. McGraw-Hill '95.

Griffin, Gerald R. Machiavelli on management. Praeger '91.

Jones Bryan D. and Bachelor, Lynn W. The sustaining hand: community leadership and corporate power. Univ. of Kansas '93.

Haig, William L. and Harper, Laurel. The power of logos. Van Nostrand Reinhold '97.

Harrison, Bennett. Lean and mean. Basic '94.

Himmelstein, Jerome L. Looking good and doing good. Indiana Univ. Press '97.

* Keller, Morton. Regulating a new economy: public policy and economic change in America, 1900-1933. Harvard Univ. Press '90.

* Mandle, Jay R. and Lou Ferleger. No pain, no gain. Twentieth Cent. Fund Press '92.

Mazzocco, Dennis W. Networks of power: Corporate TV's threat to democracy. South End '94.

Monks, Robert A. G. and Minow, Nell. Power and accountability. HarperBusiness '91.

Nader, Ralph, ed. et.al. The case against free trade: GATT, NAFTA and the globalization of corporate power. North Atlantic '93.

Labor Institute, The. Corporate power and the American dream: toward an economic agenda for working people. Apex '96.

Parkinson, J. E. Corporate power and responsibility: issues in the theory of company law. Oxford '95.

Petzinger, Thomas, Jr. Hard Landing: The epic contest for power and profits that plunged the airlines into chaos. Times '95.

* Schroth, Raymond A. The American journey of Eric Sevareid. Steerforth '95.

Thourlby, William. Passport to power. Wittenburg & Brown '90.

Tool, Marc R. and Warren J. Samuels, ed. State, society, and corporate power. Transaction '89.

Turow, Joseph. Media systems in society: understanding industries, strategies, and power. Longman '97.

Additional Periodical Articles with Abstracts

For those who wish to read more widely on the subject of corporations and corporate power, this section contain abstracts of additional articles that bear on the topic. Readers who require a comprehensive list of materials are advised to consult *Reader's Guide Abstracts* and other Wilson indexes.

Exercising our stock options. Earl G. Graves. *Black Enterprise* 28/9:9 Ap '98

African-Americans must dedicate a greater proportion of their income to corporate ownership, through the purchase of individual stocks, mutual funds, and other investment vehicles. There is power and influence, as well as an opportunity to gain wealth, in owning stock and being a corporate shareholder. It is not possible for people to will their salary to their children, but the bequeathing of stock can be the key to economic power today and wealth accumulation for generations to come.

Going beyond city limits? Municipalities are exercising their clout on social issues—and business is balking. Linda Himelstein. *Business Week* p98-9 Jl 7 '97

Local governments are passing bold laws on industry that give them a say in everything from human rights issues to compensation. Municipalities are becoming increasingly aware that they can wield power over business and adopt laws that affect how multinational corporations function. This is not the first time that cities have tried to control business, but it is reaching deeper into core corporate policy, inciting resentment from companies. Advocates of such initiatives note that cities must fill a void left by a less interventionist federal government, but opponents worry that this policy lets city hall play national politics, a role that is inappropriate and unconstitutional. A sidebar briefly discusses four areas in which local governments have passed laws to restrict the practices of businesses.

How a corporate watchdog nearly lost its bite. Robert Kuttner. *Business Week* p24 My 20 '96

A newly assertive Securities & Exchange Commission (SEC) is attempting to save the Financial Accounting Standards Board (FASB) from a recent power play by large corporations and banks that seek more latitude for creative accounting. Important business and banking leaders are opposed to the degree of disclosure that FASB champions: The FASB is working on a new standard that requires derivative securities to be counted at present market value, and, starting in 1993, the organization has sought clearer accounting of executive stock options. In April 1996, however, Arthur Levitt Jr., the SEC chairman, declared that the FASB needed more independence from business pressure rather than less. He wants a governing body of public figures and representatives of the investor community that is committed to the FASB's operating independence.

A kink in the profits pipeline. Kathleen Madigan. *Business Week* p112 Mr 2 '98

A consensus forecast of 50 economists, taken by Blue Chip Economics, predicts an increase in corporate profits of just 4.6 percent this year. Even if economic growth slows to 2.4 percent in 1998, that pace will be quick enough to create millions of new jobs and push the unemployment rate below its present 4.7 percent. The ensuing shortage of highly skilled workers will give more employees an upper hand in pay deals.

What is more, talk in Washington, D.C., of a minimum-wage rise in 1999 indicates that the upward pressure will continue into next year. At the same time, productivity will not repeat its 1.7 percent increase of 1997, according to Chris Varvares of Macroeconomics Advisers. In addition, pricing power will remain weak, particularly for manufacturers whose products compete with suddenly cheaper imports.

A pack of 800-lb. gorillas. Michael J. Mandel. *Business Week* p34-5 F 3 '97

In almost every major American industry, the number of major players is getting smaller. According to Securities Data Company, domestic mergers and acquisitions in 1996 totaled a record $659 billion, and the merger binge looks set to pick up steam in 1997. Up until now, the economic impact of the merger boom has been positive: Companies have not been able to raise prices despite increased concentration, so inflation has stayed low. In addition, corporate earnings have increased significantly, benefiting in part from merger-related efficiency gains. Nevertheless, as mergers continue and the number of competitors declines, companies, particularly in industries such as defense, railroads, and health care, will be more and more tempted to take advantage of their market power and raise prices.

Political players: who needs them on the board? John A. Byrne. *Business Week* p38 F 9 '98

It may be time to question the merits of having such a power broker as Vernon E. Jordan Jr. on a company board. Jordan is a man without equal in his specialty of making connections in Washington and working in the background to make things happen, all very discreetly. By today's standards of corporate governance, however, Jordan, who sits on ten corporate boards, including Dow Jones, Xerox, and Union Carbide, is both overextended and conflicted.

This shopping spree isn't over yet. James C. Cooper and Kathleen Madigan. *Business Week* p23-4 Ag 12 '96

The consumers' shopping spree is buoying corporate profits and the economy. The continued resilience of consumers, who purchase two-thirds of gross domestic product each quarter, is one of the main reasons why overall demand held up so well in the second quarter. On Wall Street, according to Zacks Investment Research, 57 percent of the more than 400 earnings reports announced through July 30 have been on the high side of predictions. Unemployment is exceptionally low and wages are growing quickly, although the value of benefit packages continues to decline. Moreover, for the first time in over a decade, real wages are showing sustained increases, which gives many workers more purchasing power while inflation remains low. The only potential negative in the consumer outlook for the second half is the reversal of fortune in the stock market, but unless the labor markets take a turn for the worse consumer spending should continue to be a steadfast contributor to economic growth for the rest of the year.

Corporate rule. Ed Finn. *The Canadian Forum* 74:5-6 Mr '96

Left-wing political activists must accept that Canada is no longer a democracy and turn their protests against the corporate sector where the real power lies. Corporations and other members of the upper class control the political system and set its agenda, and politicians function simply to translate corporate objectives into legislation. This system is responsible for policies that favor business and the rich, including cuts in social programs, Medicare, education, UI, and welfare, as well as shifting more of the tax burden from the rich to the middle class. Government leaders are rewarded with lucrative executive posts when they are voted out of office. Protests have not been targeted at this real seat of power for three reasons: inertia, a belief that many backbenchers can be goaded into resisting government decisions, and the few apparent successes that misleadingly point to the efficacy of appealing to politicians.

The party of corporate Canada. Richard Cleroux. *The Canadian Forum* 74:15-18 Ap '96

The Business Council on National Issues (BCNI), which represents 150 CEOs, has been a major force in directing the political agenda under the Tories and now the Liberals. With a Tory government in power, the BCNI pushed free trade and cutbacks to social programs and fueled deficit paranoia. Now, under the Liberal government of Prime Minister Jean Chretien, the BCNI has positioned itself to take a leading role in the constitutional debate. In early March, the organization and its president, Tom d'Aquino, convened a symposium entitled "Confederation 2000," which brought to Ottawa distinguished former politicians and constitutional veterans to talk about constitutional change and saving Canada. Three task force committees are scheduled to meet again over six weeks and draw up the outline of what will be a constitutional proposal to be passed at a second symposium on May 3-4 in Ottawa. The proposal will then be presented to the federal and provincial governments for their consideration. A sidebar lists the 96 most generous corporate sponsors to the Liberal Party in 1994.

Are big corporations bad for consumers? Don Matthews. *Consumers' Research Magazine* 79:25-7 My '96

An article reprinted from the February 1996 issue of The Freeman. Critics of capitalism and big corporations frequently claim that such companies have excessive economic power that they use to exploit consumers and workers. Over the past ten years, median profit as a percentage of revenue for the biggest 500 companies has ranged from 2.4 percent in 1992 to 5.5 percent in 1988, and these figures do not appear to add up to corporate exploitation of consumers. The major part of corporate income goes to workers, who received at least 90 percent of the corporate income accessible for distribution each year between 1985 and 1992. The idea that economic power is concentrated in big corporations is erroneous, as individual firms operate in their own interest and not the interests of large corporations as a group. The economic power of large corporations cannot be correctly gauged without considering the usually fierce competition between firms, and this competition curbs the power firms have over consumers and workers by punishing businesses that exploit these two groups.

Grove, Andrew S. *Current Biography* 59:18-21 Mr '98

Andrew S. Grove is the chairman, president, and CEO of Intel Corp., the Silicon Valley giant that makes nearly 90% of the microchips used worldwide to run personal computers. With $6.9 billion in earnings on revenues of $25.1 billion in 1997, the company is one of the most profitable businesses on the planet. In addition to running PCs, Intel microprocessors power a huge array of devices—everything from traffic lights to calculators, medical equipment, and electronic toys. While Grove helped to formulate microchip technology, his genius has been in applying exacting management skills and tough business practices to create the efficient corporate environment responsible for Intel's success. Grove has written three books about his fiercely competitive style of management, including *Only the Paranoid Survive: How to Exploit the Crisis Points that Challenge Every Company and Career* (1996).

Brain power: who owns it . . . how they profit from it. Thomas A. Stewart. *Fortune* 135:104-7+ Mr 17 '97

An article excerpted from *Intellectual Capital.* Corporate America is now constructed on intellectual capital rather than bricks and mortar. In the age of intellectual capitalism, the human tasks—sensing, judging, creating, building relationships—are the most valuable parts of a job. Companies, however, often manage human capital haphazardly because they find it difficult to distinguish between the cost of paying people and the value of investing in them. Moreover, compensation systems and governance structures fail to identify the owners of intellectual assets. In their effort to acquire as much human capital as they can use profitably, companies should employ an organizational rather than an individual perspective.

Get with the new power game. Thomas A. Stewart. *Fortune* 135:58-62 Ja 13 '97

Corporate power today is not what it was 20 years ago. The biggest change is that formal authority—ultimately coercive power—has changed. Knowledge work, with its dependence on project teams and cross-functional collaboration, is innately resistant to formal authority. The market's invisible influence has dealt the most telling blows to formal authority: Companies cannot be fast or global if people in the field do not possess the power to make judgment calls. Indeed the way to amass power now appears to be to give it away: The power office, for example, is passe, and the really fashionable housing for power players is now a cubicle. The writer discusses reasons for this conspicuous nonconsumption.

Appraising boardroom performance. Jay Alden Conger, David Finegold and Edward W. Lawler. *Harvard Business Review* 76:136-40+ Ja/F '98

The board of directors, one of a company's most significant contributors, is rarely subjected to an appraisal. Reviewing the performance of a board, when done correctly, can help it to become more effective by clarifying individual and collective duties. It can also help to improve the business relationship between a firm's board and its senior management and can assist in guaranteeing a healthy balance of power between the board and the CEO. Moreover, once instituted, an appraisal process is hard to dismantle, making it more difficult for a new CEO to dominate a board or escape accountability for poor performance. The writers draw on the strengths of a number of approaches to synthesize a best-practice process that is both rigorous and thorough.

The citizen corporation. Charles B. Handy. *Harvard Business Review* 75:26+ S/O '97

Part of a cover story on future business trends and emerging challenges for executives. The old language of property and ownership is an insult to democracy because it no longer describes what a company really is. The idea of a corporation as the property of its shareholders does not make clear where power lies and gives inadequate recognition to workers, a company's principal assets. A public corporation should be regarded as a community that is created by common purpose rather than common place. Although a community is something to which one belongs, it belongs to no one, a fact that has implications for the way a company is controlled. As more corporations realize that there is more to life than profits, they will become increasingly interested in enriching the lives of the workers.

Democratizing our economy. John Buell. *The Humanist* 56:37-8 Ja/F '96

The artificial scarcity of good jobs will endure until America has a political movement willing to curb the excesses of the market and democratize the economy. A response must be devised that improves the quality of life for both welfare recipients and traditional full-time office and factory workers. Given current hostility to welfare, humanists should begin with a critique of welfare for the rich and advocate a range of programs that would offer basic security and empowerment to all. The increasing difficulties of traditional liberal reforms in stemming the tide of corporate power can only lead to an intensified and ever more angry conservatism if humanists fail to keep a more democratic analysis and agenda alive. The writer proposes low-cost ways to increase the number of quality jobs and give workers more time for family and leisure pursuits.

Methods of media manipulation. Michael Parenti. *The Humanist* 57:5-7 Jl/Ag '97

America will not move forward as a nation or as a democracy unless it alerts itself to the methods of media manipulation that are inherent in the daily production of news and commentary. Media manipulation does not take place in a random fashion; rather, it moves in the same overall direction time and time again. The ingrained biases of the corporate mainstream media faithfully reflect the predominant ideology, rarely straying into territory that may cause discomfort to those who wield political and economic power, including those individuals who own the media or who advertise in it. Various means by which the media influence popular opinion are discussed.

Banking's big bang. Douglas Henwood. *The Nation* 266/15:4-5 Ap 27 '98

The proposed $70 billion merger between Citicorp and the Travelers Group to form Citigroup is illegal. Under current law, commercial and investment banking are prohibited from practicing under the same corporate roof, as are commercial banking and insurance. Citigroup would breach all these bans because Travelers is composed of an eponymous insurance company and the investment firm Salomon Smith Barney, while Citibank is a commercial bank. The theory behind the merger is that the public desires one-stop shopping for checking, life insurance, and stock trading. The instinctive populist response to the merger, however, is to oppose it on the grounds that it would make the financial system more risky and increase the concentration of wealth and power.

The new union label. David Moberg. *The Nation* 262:11-13+ Ap 1 '96

If the labor movement is to reverse its continued downward slide in relative numbers, political clout, and bargaining power, it must radically transform itself. Labor must change not only its leadership, organizational charts, and financial priorities but also the culture of unionism and even the outlook of a lot of its members. The first priority is organizing, using dramatically more aggressive and ambitious approaches to succeed against hostile employers and unfriendly laws. Achieving more power for the workers will in part mean winning the battle of ideas against the dominant corporate and right-wing interpretations of the world. The AFL-CIO executive council approved two broad initiatives on organizing and politics at its February meeting: an organizing fund to be used to encourage unions to attempt new ways of organizing, and an election-year campaign of education and organizing on issues concerning union families.

Piracy isn't what it used to be. Michael Walzer. *The New Republic* 216:29 Ap 28 '97

Piracy and modern corporate practices are compared. In the old period of pirate democracy, the near equality of shares was more than likely guaranteed by the threat of mutiny. Today, however, there would not be many mutinies, since companies would just send out replacement crews. Radical inequalities of power and wealth produce a passive and weak citizenship. Radical equalities, even if they are on the margins of the law, evoke happier adventures.

800-pound guests at the Pentagon. Leslie Wayne. *New York Times* p5 Mr 15 '98

The corporate downsizing and consolidation that have swept the military-industrial complex haven't weakened defense companies' lobbying power. Instead, the companies' power is increasing: political contributions are on the upswing, they engage the best K Street lobbyists, and they have gained the upper hand against a Pentagon that once could pit one contractor against another.

Congress uses leadership PAC's to wield power. Leslie Wayne. *New York Times* p B10 Mr 13 '97

Leadership political action committees, such as Senator Trent Lott's New Republican Majority Fund, are a backdoor way of raising money and currying congressional favor, say critics. Even though Lott was not a candidate, corporate lobbyists contributed $1.7 million to his PAC during the election campaigns in 1996. The ten largest leadership PACs associated with Republican and Democratic members of Congress, based on receipts, are listed.

A boardroom of one's own. Michael Lewis. *New York Times Magazine* p24 Mr 17 '96

Hardly an excess occurs in today's corporate America without the tacit approval of a female business executive. For example, the 1986 leveraged buyout of Macy's, which sent the company into bankruptcy, had the backing of board member Beverly Sills. Moreover, it is uncertain how far investment bankers would have gotten in the 1988 buyout of RJR Nabisco without Linda Robinson's artfully timed press releases. The writer suggests possible reasons behind women's newfound power in the business world.

Dimming the sun. Jeffrey Bartholet. *Newsweek* 129:38-9 Mr 17 '97

Government and corporate interests are now rapidly diverging in Japan. In the hyper-paced Information Age, companies must be quick, and the Japanese bureaucrat is increasingly more of a burden than a help. Japan's sputtering economy and a series of scandals have weakened the bureaucrats' reputation, even as Prime Minister Ryutaro Hashimoto discusses plans to cut their power. The high-definition television (HDTV) technology fiasco is a clear indication that their influence is fading. By using the collective strength of government and business, and billions of investment dollars, Japan planned to create a new global standard and extend its technological empire with HDTV. A recent government study determined that the real wave of the future is digital technology led by U.S. companies, and Japan is now dropping its plans to broadcast analog HDTV signals from a satellite to be launched around the turn of the century. A sidebar provides information on some of Japan's biggest industrial policy errors.

Caverns of Clinton. Matthew Rothschild. *The Progressive* 60:4 D '96

Ralph Nader's candidacy in the recent presidential election was important in that he highlighted the merits of grassroots democracy and voiced opposition to corporate power and President Bill Clinton's sellouts. Moreover, a number of leading left-wing writers exposed the moral vacuousness inherent in progressives voting for Clinton as the lesser of two evils. The large vote for Nader in Madison, Wisconsin, is discussed.

The strike of the century. David Oliver Relin. *Scholastic Update* 129:18-19 N 15 '96

The writer chronicles the armed battle fought in 1892 between the nation's most powerful union, the American Federation of Labor, and Andrew Carnegie's Carnegie Steel Company in Homestead, Pennsylvania, which resulted in the defeat of the union and ushered in a new era of corporate power.

Power and control. Wilson L. Harrell. *Success* 43:96 Je '96

The question of how many of a company's directors are elected by entrepreneurs and how many are elected by investors inevitably becomes a major bone of contention for firms. In general, whoever owns the most stock elects most members of the board, leaving the minority with no say in what takes place. Entrepreneurs who require money are frequently confronted with the cruel choice of either retaining control or staying alive. The writer offers a solution to this dilemma.

Dial M for merger. John Greenwald. *Time* 150:100-1 O 27 '97

The efforts of rival telecommunications giants to buy MCI are becoming the largest takeover battle in American corporate history. GTE Corp. chairman Charles Lee, who has offered $28 billion in cash for MCI, is now on a collision course with WorldCom CEO Bernard Ebbers, who is offering $30 billion in stock and has already broken up the long-planned $19.9 billion buyout of MCI by British Telecommunications. Not since the $25 billion war for RJR Nabisco ten years ago has a takeover battle so enlivened Wall Street. The telecom bidders want to establish empires that can offer everything from local calls to long distance to Internet access for consumers worldwide. A winning move for MCI would turn either GTE or WorldCom into the main competitor of AT&T. The battle could be decided as much by the personal styles of the CEOs as by the power of their offers.

Unleashing the power of the human mind and spirit. Earnest Deavenport. *Vital Speeches of the Day* 63:276-8 F 15 '97

On the occasion of his receipt of the Kavaler Award in Washington, D.C., the chairman and chief executive officer of Eastman Chemical Company discusses the growing anxiety among the millions of U.S. workers who feel they are being disenfranchised by capitalism and what the business community, as the champions of capitalism, must do to turn the tide of discontentment. One way the business community can stem employee discontent is to create a new socioeconomic contract with U.S. workers that will provide them with a greater share in the success of corporate America. If employees have a genuine stake in the capitalist system, if they share equally in its risks and rewards, then they will become more productive, more innovative, and more focused on creating real value.

Money and power. Harris Collingwood. *Working Woman* 22:23-5 Ja '97

A special section on powerful women executives. Although women remain poorly represented among the Fortune 500's best-paid, most powerful executives, economic consultant Nuala Beck believes women are well-placed to thrive in today's economy. Through a combination of historical accident and prescient planning, she notes, women have poured into the industries that are generating the most jobs and the biggest fortunes. Beck's belief is confirmed by a survey of the 20 top-paid women in corporate America. Four of the top 10 women and 8 of the top 20 are in fields Beck identifies as the engines driving the new economy: computers and semiconductors, health care and medicine, communications and telecommunications, and instrumentation. Related articles contain profiles of the 20 top-paid women in corporate America, a list of salary averages in a range of employment categories, and a discussion of the increasing diversity of corporate boards.

Index